MW00625395

"This book will tra
Cameron has bee~ ~ ~~~ ~~ my family. He has helped to walk and guide us through life's journey of mountains and valleys. In his powerful and transformational book, *Full House-It's Time for Household Salvation!* You too can experience what our family has gained from the wisdom and knowledge that Jesus has poured into Philip. This is your moment to restore your family legacy and rebuke the enemy out of your home. I truly believe this book will be a classic for generations! It is time to populate heaven and depopulate hell!"

"Philip Cameron is a great friend and a wonderful servant of God. His book *Full House – It's Time for Household Salvation!* Is a great read from a man who is living it. The Gospel that Philip is preaching is changing people's lives. He is having a great effect on ending human trafficking in the world and he is transforming the lives of those he rescues. After they are released, they become great Christians who are having a positive impact on the world. I celebrate his courage and this new generation he is raising from his own biological children to the ones who become his spiritual children through his ministry The Orphan's Hands."

"This is how the story goes... I love a good story. I love Philip Cameron's story. His heritage is worthy. His life is inspirational. Not because of what he has gained but by what he has given. He has given his life so that others can rewrite their stories. You will be inspired as you read, *Full House – It's Time for Household Salvation!* By Philip Cameron. You will want to invite others into your own story, into your house, to sit at your table where conversation, yes even communion of laughter and even tears are part of the story. Enjoy."

–Neil Kennedy, Author,
Founder and President, FivestarMan

"I first met Philip Cameron in 1970. He was with his father Simon Peter and his mother Wendy. They had come from Scotland to Nova Scotia, Canada with "Dancing Hearts" and brought a mighty move of the Spirit! A very close bond was formed back then that lasts till this day.

Years past, I was now pastoring Queensway Cathedral in Toronto, Canada. My wife Evelyn and I were visiting Charlotte, North Carolina walking down Main Street USA, at PTL, where The Jim Bakker show was produced. I literally bumped into Philip who was appearing on the show. We spoke, reminisced about the years gone by and felt once again the bond that had been struck over 20 years before. I invited Philip to speak at our church, he accepted and unknown to us, history was about to be made.

My brother in law David Mainse was the host of 100 Huntley Street a television program seen across Canada and the USA. Philip had been invited to be on David's show but hadn't filled out the paperwork to appear. He was canceled. Philip was in my office when I learned of the cancellation. I immediately called David. I asked if he had a pen to write a note. I waited till he did. "Write this down David. Today I blew it." When David asked me why, I told him of the move of God we were experiencing at Queensway. Philip was on 100 Huntley Street the next day.

What happened next was miraculous. Towards the end of the program, David asked Philip what God had been speaking to him about. Philip asked a single question. "How much is your daughter's soul worth? I'll give you a billion dollars to turn to the camera and say my daughter doesn't have to be in heaven with me." David began to weep. Philip turned to his camera, and made a statement that lit a fuse that exploded across North America. "It's time for Household Salvation!" "I want to pray for your loved ones to be saved, call now and let me believe with you." Every phone in the building began to ring at once. Then, they went silent. They were jammed.

As he left the building, the producers who had canceled him the day before were following him to the door, arranging for a return visit. He did. For six weeks. During that time, the phone banks at Huntley Street stayed jammed with approximately three million names of unsaved loved ones being called in for prayer.

One call moved us all. It was from an Inuit Village, far in the north of Canada. The woman gave the names of her family in her tribe. She was weeping, concerned if she had left out a single name from the list. It was a revival of Household Salvation!

Philip then spoke across all Canada on two separate tours; an average of 10% of every audience gave their hearts to Christ.

Oral Roberts invited Philip to share his vision in Tulsa, Oklahoma. The phone lines in the Prayer Tower at ORU jammed. So many names were called in. A special altar was built to hold the almost one million names sent in for prayer!

I witnessed these things personally. My dear brother in law David has passed on to Glory but he never forgot the season when Heaven kissed the earth, and the Heart of the Father was revealed in His passion for SOULS! This revival is needed now more than ever. We all should cry to have a "Full House" when Jesus calls or comes. You are about to have your life changed!"

–Ralph Rutledge, Author, Missionary

FULL HOUSE

It's Time for Household Salvation!

Philip Cameron

Dedication

There is an old saying, "The hand that rocks the cradle, rules the world." This book is dedicated to moms. First, my own mother, Wendy Cameron who rocked my cradle and for the cause of Christ ruled my world. She created an atmosphere of love for me, for Jesus, and for the world! Through her life and testimony, she shaped my thoughts to see the value of serving. Her hands led me to Christ and into the Gospel.

For Chrissie, the girl who rocked the cradles of our four children, Philip, Melody, Andrew, and Lauren and who today is rocking our grandbabies. Chrissie let me dream, see the invisible, and pursue after the call of God in my life. For more than 25 years, she has rocked the cradles of so many orphans. In her own quiet way, her love has been manifest in the care shown to those who have never found the safety of a mom: memorizing their shoe sizes, favorite color, the style of clothes they prefer and her endless search for "bargains." Chrissie has been called Mom by countless kids who today, live in all the corners of the world. From Israel to Australia, her hand is seen; her love is manifest in the salvation of so many.

Contents

Foreword

There seldom comes a resource that speaks so directly to issues facing the family in today's society: especially giving the honor due in the homes led by praying mothers and how God honors those prayers and saves those with the hardest hearts in one's own family. The personal testimonies and transparency of Philip Cameron of how God saved his own parents and grandparents from destruction is nothing short of supernatural. If you have a family member that has yet to come to Christ, then, this book is a must read for you.

The godly wisdom revealed by Philip Cameron in this writing is priceless. Anyone in a family where others have yet to come to Christ will greatly benefit by this incredible and encouraging book. It is obvious that the greatest weapon the enemy uses is discouragement that a family member will never come to Christ, which is exactly what my dear friend Philip Cameron set himself to dislodge. This book will help you successfully navigate the terrain of: praying for lost loved ones and then watch as God touches hearts and changes lives.

–Marcus D. Lamb, Founder – President Daystar
Television Network

Introduction

We live in perilous times. On one hand, we are prosperous. On the other, there is a seemingly unstoppable wave of compromise. It often seems that the Church has lost touch with the pertinent realities of life, while nations and continents slide toward doom. So many people are caught up with the cosmetics of Christianity, rather than facing and correcting the terrible problems that, if left unsolved, will destroy not only the Church, but the world.

Christians are the earth's salt, the essence of real life in an unreal world. We are God's examples—epistles known and read by those with whom we share our lives. But somewhere, we have failed in that responsibility. I am disturbed—no, dismayed—by our apparent inability to maintain a generation to generation flow of the truth and promise of God. In this book I intend, with the help of God, to shed light and give hope to the mother, father, spouse, child, and anyone else who yearns to see the lost members of his or her family come to Jesus.

In this generation, the family is under more pressure to break apart than at any other time in history. As people must try harder to survive in the rat-race, more and more become unable to cope with the dual responsibilities of work and parenthood fully. Children who already live in a sin-wracked society are given more time and more money to themselves, and thus, they become prime targets of satanic attacks. It is a fact that the decline of the family has played a significant part in the demise of every great civilization. We, in this generation, simply do not have time to waste, if we are to act to prevent Satan from claiming the eternal souls of our loved ones.

I intend to show you that God is indeed able to act in your family's situation. As you read about the experience of the Cameron Family, and then to go on to discover the extent of the promises of Household Salvation in God's words, I trust that you will be challenged to begin the process of winning your entire family to Jesus. Let me tell you now, no one in your family is beyond the reach of grace. No matter how evil or dark the world in which they live, there is no power, no demons, no family history that can compare to the power of Jesus and the Gospel. So, let's get one thing clear now. Your unsaved loved ones are candidates for the Cross.

It is time to make a stand, to break from our death-dealing lethargy. I pray that this small contribution will help someone to rise with the tide of God and say, "IT'S TIME TO CLAIM THE UNCLAIMED PROMISE - HOUSEHOLD SALVATION!"

Part I

Chapter One
The Camerons

—⚭—

The part of the Cameron clan from which I come is typical of many families in Scotland and around the world. There was a total lack of knowledge of who Jesus is and what He could do. We had *just never heard.* Therefore, the darkness of sin dominated every aspect of Cameron life. That darkness can take many forms. It was alcoholism in our family. How we lived was completely normal to us. Generations of my family were bound in the vicious cycle of drunkenness, seemingly with no end in sight.

Maybe your loved ones are the same. Their way of life is normal to them, and they think you are the one that is crazy. You go to church, "give your money to the preacher," some may talk in tongues and lift your hands, speak about "the blood" and what "the Lord told you." They do not understand the love relationship between you and Jesus.

But God is a wonder-worker and is, as Scripture states, "not willing that any should perish" (2 Peter 3:9). In our situation, we had no personal contact with the Gospel, so God had to arrange a meeting. In His mercy, He showed His love to our sin-laden family. The whole thought process of God's heart is Household Salvation. He never slumbers or sleeps, so when we put our heads on our pillows at night, the heart, the mind and the hand of God are at work. There is no distance; there is no time zone, there is no geographical location where His Love is not already present and working. God is a family man. He knows how it feels to have lost a son. And He is thinking and planning for you to say, like the Prodigal's father, "My son was dead and is alive again." NOTHING is beyond His reach!

I call them "anointed moments." They are marvelous encounters between God and man. We see such moments in Eden's Garden when God communed with Adam and Eve and at the temple when Simeon and Anna beheld the Christ child. These special times when God reaches down to touch a human heart have always occurred, and, as long as this dispensation of Grace lasts, they always will. The heart of the Father continually longs for the restoration of fellowship with fallen man. The "anointed moment" for your loved ones is on its way. Just the fact that you are holding this book in your hand is a divine indicator that something is happening in the Spirit. The interest that made you pick it up is a cry from your heart to God, and I want you to know this: When you call. He is going to answer.

Dream with me a little. It's Sunday morning, and you are sitting in church, and all around you are the very ones you are praying for today. Get this faith-picture in your spirit: As the songs of praise rise, they are worshiping God, redeemed.

I don't care where they are right now. I know where God wants them, and His arm is not too short to save them, and that is how my story begins.

The Town Drunk

My Father, Simon Peter Cameron, was the youngest of seven children born to Michael and Christina Cameron. Christina came from the extreme northwest of Scotland and spoke Gaelic, the original language of my homeland. Like many other Highland girls, she followed the fishing fleet from port to port. These were strong young women who made their livelihood packing the fish into barrels and boxes.

She met my grandfather while working in the fish industry in Peterhead. By that time, Grandfather had already inherited the curse of the Camerons ~ he was an alcoholic. When he was barely seventeen, he had lied about his age to join the army during the World War I. In many horrible battles, he saw the lives of most of his friends snuffed out, one by one, as they clambered out of the muddy trenches into a hail of bullets. Only a handful of young men returned to our part of Scotland.

The troops were given rum and whiskey to instill false courage, and Michael always got his share. Eventually, he was sent home with shrapnel wounds in the head and back, suffering from dysentery, and trapped by an even more dangerous affliction—alcohol bound him. He promised Christina that his drinking was a thing of the past, but that pledge of sobriety was forgotten almost as soon as they were married. His addiction to alcohol lasted over forty years. Many times, while on a drunken spree, my grandfather would end up completely paralyzed by liquor, and he would disappear for up to six weeks at a time. Sometimes they would find him lying in the street with his arms wrapped around his two dogs, Fanny and Flossy. Only their body heat kept him from freezing to death.

My father remembers one occasion when Grandfather had sneaked out of his bedroom window with his new suit ~ a rare luxury ~ under his arm. He planned to sell it for enough money to buy more drinks. But on that occasion, my grandmother intercepted him. Her stubborn will, forged in the fires of necessity, prevailed and they hung the suit back in the closet.

Raising seven children whose ages spanned less than twelve years in the nineteen-twenties and thirties was difficult at best, but the problem of drunkenness made the situation nearly impossible. There was little enough money anyway, and every shilling spent on drink added to the difficulties.

My grandmother found unusual ways of augmenting the family income. They lived within a stone's throw of the North Sea, and when the fishing boats docked at the pier with their catches, Grandmother would be waiting. When fish fell out of the boxes, as men unloaded the ships, she would gather them. With her basket full of fish, she walked many miles into the countryside, visiting the farms that surrounded the town. At farm after farm, she would knock on the doors and offer the fish for sale or barter. Only great need forced this shy girl from the Hebrides to do this, but she was determined to keep her family together and to meet their needs. She was barely able to do so, and in those desperate days, there was little or no hope of ever improving what seemed to be an unchangeable situation.

An Anointed Moment

War swept over all of Europe in 1939, even reaching to the ports of northern Scotland. The eldest son of Michael and Christina Cameron, Michael Jr., went to work for the British Iron and Steel Corporation. The United States had not yet entered the war, but was supplying lease-lend materials to Great Britain to help in the war effort. Their ships became targets for Nazi air and submarine attacks. When the ships were hit, the brave men would try to salvage the cargo and even the metal of the ship itself.

A ship had been beached on the Island of Stroma, one of the small islands off the coast of Scotland. Young Michael was part of the crew assigned to salvage the vessel. Stroma lies just over a mile from the mainland, and although deserted today, it was once a thriving community of many families. Michael lodged at one of the farms on the island.

Although he was only in his late teens, Michael had already followed in his father's footsteps ~ he was under the bondage of alcohol and was well known on the island for his drinking habits. While he was stationed on Stroma, he would take advantage of any leave to go over to the mainland for liquor. The only means of transportation available was a small boat owned by an old man with one leg, who would row passengers over and back for a shilling. Michael would get drunk and then return to Stroma with as many bottles of alcohol as he could carry. The backward "Heelan folk" of Stroma, with their strong Calvinist roots, were horrified at the raucous young men from the lowlands that had invaded their island to break the Americans' boat.

On one such trip to the mainland, Michael left the boat intending to purchase a supply of liquor, but ended up with much more than he had expected. Something happened that was to change the entire path of the Cameron family. He walked into a small café, which also served as the bus stop in that small village, for a cup of tea. As he waited for the bus and the waitress to bring his order, his glance fell on a small piece of paper wedged between the salt and pepper shakers. Reaching over, he picked it up and began to read.

He read about the Creator and man, sin, and bondage. He felt like the author had been writing about Michael, himself. He read on, to learn about Jesus coming to Earth, about the manger and the love shown at Calvary, and the grace of God demonstrated. Then, the "anointed moment" came. Suddenly, the revelation of grace dawned on his sin-sick heart. He was keenly aware of his sin and his shame, and in total simplicity, he rolled his burden onto Jesus.

God had broken through! A beachhead was established in the Cameron family. The young man, who had left Stroma Island a sinner, had come face-to-face with the love of God.

Michael looked up at the waitress while holding the tract with trembling hands and tears began to flow. She looked down at the young man and asked THE question: "Son, are you saved?" He had never been in church and had never heard the Gospel. He had never heard the term "saved" before, but he knew his life had changed. He would never be the same.

"Yes." He replied.

He went on to ask her, "Where are these words from?"

"It's the Bible, Son: God's book to mankind."

"Where can I get one of these Bibles?" he asked. She pointed in the direction of Wick, the place he had been heading to get drunk, "There is a small reading room underneath the Kirk o' Scotland (the Church of Scotland). They sell them, and you can get one there."

The bus couldn't drive fast enough for Michael. He ran through to the place she told him about, in the small north-of-Scotland town. He ran down the stairs, put his money on the desk and as keenly as he had ever ordered a scotch or a beer, Michael Cameron said, "I want Bibles." All his money was gone, but wrapped in brown paper, tucked tightly under his arms was the source of his redemption. He got back on the bus, back on the rowing boat, and crossed the mile to Stroma.

He knocked on every door of the tiny island and told everyone on the island Who he had just found.

As a footnote to this day: Decades later, a team of young people from our church in Scotland was evangelizing, and knocked on a door in a village on the mainland, called Longside. An old woman came to the door and listened to our young people. As they spoke, she said, "Hold on a minute." She reappeared holding a Bible that a nineteen-year-old boy called Michael

Cameron on the island of Stroma had given her family. He had signed his name inside.

Michael's mind turned to Peterhead and home – his family had to know! Jesus would do the same for them! As he got on the bus in the town of Wick, the same town where he bought the Bibles, his mind raced with excitement. "My family will be so pleased to hear. Dad will be different."

Michael, in his new-found faith, did not realize what was ahead for him – seven years in which he would stand alone against the ridicule of his family.

He thought it would take forever to reach his hometown of Peterhead. As he climbed those familiar steps to the kitchen of the Cameron home, his heart was racing with joy. He was ready to share his story – he couldn't wait to see the reaction of those he loved. He dropped his small cardboard suitcase at his feet and stood with his raincoat folded over his arm. He began to talk, speaking to everyone at once, telling of the great things that had taken place in his heart. He told the family of the café, the gospel tract, the grace, the forgiveness, the joy, and the peace. It poured from him in an emotional torrent. And then he told them that the good news was for them, too! Things didn't have to be the way they had been for so long. There was a better way! God could deliver them, and set them free!

Instead of a joyful reception, Michael was met with a stony silence. Each member of the family was baffled by this strange thing that had happened to their son and brother. The Bible says, *"The god of this world hath blinded the minds of them which believe not"* (2 Corinthians 4:4), and that was certainly true of the Cameron family. Instead of seeing the wonder of what had happened to Michael, they wondered what was wrong with him!

You would think that someone who was in bondage would grasp at any opportunity to be free. No matter how stupid the idea might seem to be, it would be worth a try. People, however, do not always think that way.

Michael Jr. had left Stroma Island and was working at home again. Each day at lunch time, he would come home, quickly gulp down his lunch, and then go into his bedroom to pray. Michael had received a promise from the Lord: "If you remain faithful, I will save your whole family." Michael was convinced that God would break the power of sin, and fulfill His promise of Household Salvation. My father told me many times, as he left to return to school from his lunch break, he would hear his brother Michael cry out to God as he walked past the doorway. "That's my brother Simon. Please Lord save my brother Simon." This left an indelible mark on my father's life.

In those days, long before television, families entertained themselves by sitting around the coal fire, singing songs or telling stories to pass a long winter's night that would grip the Northeast of Scotland for months at a time. On one such occasion someone asked Michael to sing a song in his strong, sweet voice. He rose to sing. Time stood still. The dim flicker of the gas mantle, with its low hiss, was accompanied by the slow tick-tock of the clock on the mantlepiece and the crackle of the coal fire. He looked around the room at his family's faces and the ache of desire to see them saved was almost overwhelming. He cleared his throat, hooked his thumbs under the straps of his overalls. This was Michael's chance. In his clear tenor voice, he began to sing. The family had expected to hear one of his many secular songs. But instead came the words, "On a hill far away stood an old rugged cross, the emblem of suffering and shame…" When he came to the verse that says, "To that old rugged cross I will ever be true, its shame and reproach gladly bear," Michael broke down and left. He returned to his bedroom in tears.

The rest of the family, feeling extremely uncomfortable, decided that this simply had to stop. Michael was going insane! They had to try to snap him out of whatever this "thing" was that had come over him. Their efforts failed. For seven long, lonely years young Michael prayed, holding to God for the fulfillment of the promise: "Remain faithful, and I will save your whole family."

During those years my Grandfather continued to drink, and eventually, his business began to deteriorate. Things got so bad that he made a promise to God: "Save my business, and I will serve you." The financial crisis passed – and so did the promise, Granddad continued in the same old ways.

Chapter Two
Love at First Sight

—⁓⁓—

Simon Peter ~ my father ~ was a teenager, was the youngest of the family and just about to leave school. He was known as "Professor," because he was always at the top of his class. He was frequently urged to continue to university, but with the self-destructive hopelessness that was typical of the Camerons in those days, he declined. He knew there was no money, and therefore no point in trying to continue. Instead, he went to work with his dad and his brothers in the junk metal business.

Despite his good marks in school, he had a very low sense of self-worth. He was the youngest of seven children, had always worn other people's castoffs and worst of all, was the son of the town drunk.

One night, Dad joined his brothers Alex and John at a dance. I realize this sounds like a cliché movie script, but he saw her across the dance floor. Her name was Wendy. She was a red-head and was laughing and enjoying herself as she danced in someone else's arms.

Eventually, Dad plucked up enough courage to ask her to dance. By the end of the evening, the sixteen-year-old lad was head over heels in love with that vivacious redhead.

Wendy was eighteen and a pharmacist's apprentice. She and her sister, Christian, had lived with their uncle Lionel and their grandmother since their parents had divorced when Wendy was six. In his mid-thirties, Lionel married and his new wife, Yolande, became a close friend to her new niece.

To Dad's surprise, Wendy was willing to continue to see him. To his utter amazement, she returned his love. For the first time in his life, he was at the center of someone's attention instead of being at the end of a line of seven. As they walked hand in hand one night, Wendy asked, "How old are you?"

"Guess," challenged Dad.

"Nineteen?"

Dad smiled. "Close," he said, enjoying the fact that she took him at his word. Even today we tease our mother that, if Dad said the moon was made of green cheese, she'd have believed it.

His age was not his only embarrassment in the growing relationship. Eventually, Mum asked him, "What kind of business is your family in?" Ashamed to admit that they bought and sold junk metal and old clothes (in Scotland the term is "rag and bone merchant"), Dad replied, "Do you know what a spirit-level is?"

Wendy nodded.

"Well, we make the little bubbles that float in the fluid to tell whether a wall is level." Again, she believed him (Let me note that while Dad could always pull this off, I have never had that effect on my Mother. From birth to now, she has been able to see straight through me, sometimes sensing my moods and needs all the way across the Atlantic Ocean).

Wendy continued to love dancing. Although her new aunt, Yolande, did not go to dances or even approve of them, she would iron Wendy's dress and clean her shoes, which allowed the young girl to rush through supper and leave immediately for the dance.

One night, Wendy rushed in, late from another long day at the pharmacy. Missing supper, she ran to where Yolande was and stood in her petticoat, waiting for the dress that was being so carefully and lovingly ironed by her new Italian auntie. As the iron, smoothed the linen fabric, a thought crossed the young redhead's mind, "Auntie Yollie, if you don't approve of me going dancing, why do you help me by ironing my dress?" Yolande laid down the old heavy iron on the board, and as she smoothed the next wrinkle needing ironing, she looked up at her niece.

The "moment" was about to be planted in Wendy's heart.

"Wendy, you're right. I don't approve of worldly things."

She continued, "This is your Heaven. It's the only Heaven you will ever know. If this is all there is going to be for you, I want you to enjoy it."

Wendy's heart sank. She grabbed the dress, quickly buttoned up the many buttons, grabbed her coat and rushed to the dance hall. As the music played and she swept across the floor, she couldn't shake the thought from her mind. "Is this all there is?" she asked herself, "Is this it? Is this my Heaven? There must be more."

That night, in the little dance hall just outside Peterhead, God had begun the winding of the line attached to her soul. Two lives, miles apart, were heading to the cross.

Crisis

Dad and Mum's love for each other grew and deepened, and despite family opposition, they began to plan and dream together. She would be a pharmacist; he somehow would make good, although, to anyone looking on, his task was formidable at best. And just when things seemed to be getting better, the bottom fell out of their world. Dad stood shivering in the cold winter night; his eyes fixed on a window of the house across the street. The cold was forgotten, for he was much more concerned with what was happening inside that house.

Finally, the red door opened, and Wendy emerged, slowly slipping her purse over her shoulder and walking, with her head bowed, toward her sixteen-year-old boyfriend. The moment that their eyes finally met, he knew without words that their world, already bleak, was now destroyed. Wendy was going to have a baby.

She was brave in the face of the disaster, and as he walked her home, she offered to go it alone. He was too young to be married, and if he wanted to be free, that was all right with her.

Simon was determined to marry his Wendy, but his parents were completely opposed to the marriage. He told them of their plight that night, and his mother put her foot down, hard – he was too young, needed their approval, and wasn't going to get it.

From the flurry of emotions that besieged the overpowered young man, one thought emerged: "If I can't have Wendy as my wife, I'd be better off dead." He knew where to find the full bottle of pills, and he dumped the entire contents into his hand. Sipping water between every few tablets, he had soon swallowed them all.

His first thought was, "I've got to see Wendy one more time." He ran out of the front door, and all the way to her home. Her guardians still knew nothing of what happened – she had been afraid to tell them because they had never had much time for this boy from the wrong side of the tracks.

Glancing from the window, Wendy saw her young, frightened boyfriend beckoning her outside. But as they spoke, he did not tell her what he had done. They talked softly and held each other close. As Dad began to feel the effect of the pills, he quickly said goodbye. He longingly watched as she turned and went into her house – he had lost everything. There was no hope. He turned homeward, wanting only to climb into his bed, and to die.

How he managed to make it all the way home is still a mystery. He was dizzy and very ill. He lunged through the door, raced into the bathroom and was violently sick. As he vomited, he thought, "I'll just have to die here."

The next thing he knew; his mother was kneeling beside him. In his haste, he had forgotten to lock the bathroom door, and she had rushed in after him. She realized what her broken-hearted son had done, and she began to weep.

Dad had never seen his mother cry. All those years of having to be a mother, father, and provider for her seven children had hardened her. But kneeling on the bathroom floor, she was broken, to my father's astonishment. She said, "I love you, Simon. I don't want to lose you. If Wendy means this much to you, then I will give you permission to get married."

The vomiting had saved his life, so that immediate danger was over.

After speedy arrangements between the two families, the time for the wedding was at hand. Simon and Wendy were married on January 24th, 1948.

Dad sat shivering and nervous in the car, which was headed for the small Registrar's office where the civil wedding ceremony would be performed. Hectic days and weeks had passed since that terrifying night in which near-tragedy had turned into a parent's blessing.

The quickly planned wedding was an added strain on the Cameron family, for Dad's older brother, John, was to be married soon after Dad and Mum's wedding.

John and his bride-to-be had received many more gifts than Simon and Wendy. Their hurried event gave little time for basic planning, let alone for wedding gifts. But one night, as the wedding dates drew near, some friends brought a gift of dishes to John. He wasn't there, so grandmother thanked the givers on behalf of her son ~ and then placed them carefully beside the few items that her youngest son, Simon, had received. Several more gifts were "liberated" in this way. Until now, no one has known of this except my father.

In the car with Dad, on the way to the Registrar's, was his eldest sister, Chrissie. She fussed over her young brother's clothes, smoothed his hair, and gave a multitude of last minute instructions, all of which fell on deaf ears. Dad was thinking only of his Wendy. But suddenly, he heard Chrissie ask a question he hadn't heard before: "Do you have enough money for the marriage license?"

His blank stare changed in an instant to one of panic. "Oh, no!" cried the startled bridegroom. "I don't have any money!"

Chrissie shook her head, imagining the disasters that this day seemed bound to produce. But then she rummaged through her purse until she found the necessary one-pound note, which she thrust into her brother's hand.

A relationship that began as a night at a dance had resulted in a hastily arranged marriage. The young couple had no money, no home - and no future. Another generation of Camerons began with all the dice loaded against them. The one thing Dad and Mum did have was love. Even living in his parent's crowded home did not diminish the enjoyment they derived from one another's company. And the ability to laugh was always part of their love.

Each day brought them closer to the birth of their baby. At night, as they lay in the darkness, they would talk about the future, and make great plans. They promised each other that, "This baby will have a better chance than we did." They were determined to give this new Cameron all the things that the Camerons had not known.

"What will we call our wee one?" Mum would ask. Dad would always respond, "If it's a boy, we'll call him Simon Alan." They were sure it would be a boy.

One day, Mum greeted Dad with a secretive smile, and said, "Simon, why don't you come up to Uncle Lionel's tonight after work? I have a surprise for you." Dad knew Mum well enough that he didn't question her, he simply showed up ~ and "surprise" was not adequate to describe his reaction.

"Follow me," beamed Wendy, and she led him through her Aunt and Uncle's house, out the back door and into the garden, to a small wooden garden shed. That shed, which measured six by twelve feet, was now furnished as a tiny home. Mum had hunted for the furniture and had somehow found a couch-bed, a small table with two chairs, a skinny wardrobe, and a throw-rug. There was a tiny wood stove in one corner. With the magic touch of love, she had somehow turned a garden shed into a home. The young couple ran an extension cord to the shed and hung one single light in the room.

On the door, Wendy had written in yellow paint: "Simon and Wendy's Hut." They moved in that night.

Excitement grew right along with Mum's tummy. But though she was bigger every day, Mum's pace did not lag. She was healthy and eager for the birth of her firstborn. The baby was to be born at Simon's parents' home, under the care of a wonderful and brilliant doctor, a man who was to play an important part in Simon and Wendy's life.

My father always had a low pain threshold ~ for his pain, and for anyone else's, as well. On one occasion, while we were vacationing in Wales, I fell and split my head open. They summoned the local doctor. When he arrived at the campsite at which we were staying, he realized that he had left his surgical needle and thread at home. He casually asked if there were a regular needle and thread available.

At this, Dad lunged toward the wardrobe, which happened to contain the sewing equipment, and began to rummage furiously. Soon a shoe flew back over his shoulder, followed immediately by its mate.

"Simon," said Mother, "I know exactly where it is. Let me look."

Father shot a frenzied glance back at his wife. "Wendy," he exclaimed, "I'm not looking for the needle. I want my coat!" With that, he was off. Despite the crisis at hand, everyone, even the doctor, could not hold back their laughter.

Dad had the same kind of struggles when it was time for the baby to be born. When Mum gave the first indication of labor, Dad began to panic. The rest of the family teased him that the doctor would have to treat him before caring for the mother and child!

When the pains were frequent enough, they called the doctor, but Dad left before the doctor arrived. He ran out, "borrowed" a neighbor's bike, and made his escape. As he pedaled away, he noticed that the wind, which usually blew in from the sea, was gusting strongly from inland, impeding his process. "Just my luck! Even the wind is against me," he thought, as he struggled to reach the crest of the hill.

Little did he foresee the real storm that was looming on his horizon. It was a breach birth. The good doctor worked very hard to make this first birth as easy as possible for the young girl he had known for years, and of whom he was very fond. After a great struggle, Simon Alan Cameron was born, a seven-pound boy. A tired, aching mother waited for her husband to return.

Simon entered the house, brave now that the struggle was over!

"He's the most beautiful baby in the world," he declared. "Wendy, he looks just like me!"

Wendy smiled. Although little Simon Alan had been born in difficult circumstances, he would be loved. He would have a better life than they had known. The doctor ordered complete bed rest until she recovered from the difficult birth. Although temporarily confined to bed, her mind was as active as ever, and her thoughts raced ahead to the happy days to come.

The baby was three days old, and Mum was beginning to feel much better. She was impatiently waiting for the first opportunity to go out and walk down the street in our town, to proudly show off her little bundle of joy. The baby was warm and soft in her arms, as she held the bottle gently in his tiny mouth.

But her day-dreaming stopped as she looked down at her son. He had stopped sucking, and immediately, she knew something was wrong. Fighting back panic, she nudged the nipple up and down to get a response, but there was none.

"Simon," she screamed, "Something's wrong with the baby!" As she spoke, she tore open her nightdress and held the wee baby close to her warm body ~ the eighteen-year-old girl wanted to give her warmth to her son, somehow thinking this would make him well.

"Get the doctor! My baby's not breathing right!"

The young father's heart felt as though it would burst, as he once again struggled to pedal up that steep hill. The "borrowed" bike did not seem to respond to his furiously pumping legs. The doctor who had delivered the baby was not close at hand, and Dad rushed to the office of the nearest doctor, even though he was a stranger to the Cameron family. Impelled by panic and fear, he rushed straight through the waiting room, right into the doctor's office. Through his tears, Dad blurted, "Doctor, come quickly! My baby's dying!"

Enraged, the doctor ordered him out of the room. "I'm with a patient! Wait until I've finished. Anyway, if it's as bad as you say, the child is probably dead by now!"

Simon waited for what seemed to be an eternity in the corridor outside the office. Finally, from the doorway, he heard the doctor give some instructions to his patient about taking some cough medicine. He then turned to the weeping young man.

"Now, what's your problem?" asked the annoyed physician. "And besides, am I your doctor?"

"No," gasped Dad, "I came here because you were closest for my baby," Dad told him the name of their family doctor.

The man turned back into his office. "I can't come, but I will call your doctor." Before he dialed the phone, he snapped at Dad, "Go home! He'll be there as soon as he can."

Dad left the office. He turned the bicycle homeward, terrified of what would be waiting for him.

Upon reaching the top of the hill, he saw the doctor's black car parked haphazardly in the street outside the house. The presence of the medical man sparked hope in the heart of the newly turned seventeen-year-old father.

But this hope was empty. Mum had been rocking the limp baby in her arms. A tiny trickle of water ran from the infant's nose. Through her tears, she called out to God, "Please don't take my baby!" But despite the diligent efforts of the doctor, he could not save the child. He was dead. Three days of joy had turned into a nightmare beyond anything the young couple could have imagined.

The storm had come. Wendy longed for the impossible – to see her baby again. Simon began to harden, as bitterness filled the void that Simon Alan had left.

The tiny white coffin covered with a white cloth was laid on the table. The young couple sat numb as the preacher led the funeral service. Mum felt as if the book of her life had been slammed shut. And at that moment, Dad's brother and his wife brought in their week-old baby to visit, which was almost too much.

At the end of the service, they got into the taxi for the ride to the grave. The undertaker laid the small coffin on Dad's knees as they drove to the cemetery. In one short year, Dad had learned to love, had almost died at his own hand, had married, had seen the birth of his baby, and then – this. He could hardly bring himself to leave the open grave.

It is said that "time heals all wounds." To a certain measure, that is right. Slowly, things began to return to normal. But there were nights when Mum would awaken, screaming, as she dreamed of the baby lying limp in her arms. Or as she watched her sister-in-law cradle her own little girl, the baby would become Simon Alan, in Mum's mind. Her longing for her child remained for many years, but in the back of Mum's mind was a strange assurance: "My baby is in Heaven."

And all this time, Dad's brother Michael was praying faithfully, every day, for Household Salvation to come to the Camerons.

Chapter Three
Married to A Stranger

—〜〜—

World War II had recently ended, but already, trouble was brewing in Korea. The mounting tensions meant that National Service was still in force, and when Simon reached the age of eighteen, he was drafted. For the young couple, this seemed disastrous. How could they live without each other for two years?

Dad endured boot camp at a place called Ellesmere. He and Wendy would write, sharing everything that was happening in their very separate lives, as the weeks and months dragged by.

Finally, Mum couldn't stand the separation any longer. On impulse, she caught the train and left Peterhead to join her husband. There were no allowances for married couples at boot camp, so Mum found lodgings with a nearby family. She took a part-time job, but spent every available minute with Dad. There were strict rules prohibiting civilians from being on army property, but where there is a will, there's a way!

In the evening, under cover of darkness, Dad would smuggle Mum into his barracks, where he shared a room with a corporal. He would cover the window with a thick, coarse blanket from his bed, and sit and watch while Wendy shined his boots, polished his brass, and cleaned his bed space. This labor of love earned Private Cameron top marks for his appearance, and his fellow soldiers never discovered the advantage he had over them.

Their time in Ellesmere was marvelous, but when boot camp ended, the time for separation came again. While the units all around him were sent to Korea, Dad's unit was posted to a multinational force in Trieste, in Northern Italy.

That change in residence led to a more serious internal change in Simon. Away from home for the first time, he began to drink, and the pattern of drunkenness which had plagued the Camerons began to emerge. Instead of avoiding the terrible bondage of alcohol, Dad fell completely into the trap. His language deteriorated, and was soon so vile that his blasphemous use of Jesus' name caused a corporal to comment,

"Cameron, I don't mind you cursing, but must you use the name of Jesus with every second breath?"

At home, Michael Jr. was still praying, eagerly awaiting the day his family would be saved. Seven years had passed since that moment in the café, but the promise had been given, and Michael was faithful. He often preached to a small congregation of about twelve people in a little church in Peterhead called the Tin Mission, due to the entire building ~ walls and ceiling ~ beings made of corrugated tin.

Michael's Reward

Two recent graduates from a Bible school in England were about to hold the very first Gospel Campaign. They had picked Peterhead as their launching point, and the services were to be held in a small room, up some stairs and around the back of a house on Broad Street. While they were in Peterhead, their home was a small, antiquated van ~ sort of a primitive motorhome, with the emphasis very much on "primitive."

These two young evangelists, Herbert Harrison and Donald Walker, did not know what was about to happen. Michael Cameron did not realize what was about to happen, either. But God knew! They had planned a brief crusade, but it lasted six weeks. There were ninety-six converts, and more than sixty of them were named Cameron! The young men didn't know what to think as, each night, convert after convert gave the same name: "Cameron."

The Camerons were coming to Jesus!

Unlike her husband, my mother had always attended church. Yet, in almost eighteen years of church services, she had never heard the Gospel! While she believed in God – the God to whom she had prayed as her baby was dying – she had never known Him as her personal Savior.

Chrissie, Simon's sister, needed help. Mum thought that a little religion would straighten her sister-in-law's life out. "Let's go and hear the preachers tonight, Chrissie," Mum suggested.

"Okay," Chrissie replied, "I have nothing else to do."

They climbed the stairs and sat down in the tiny room where so many of the Camerons had been getting saved. Mum was immediately shocked! Donald Walker was singing, and worse, he was smiling! He looked happy! This could not be a proper church service. Where was the organ? Where were the candles? Some people were even clapping their hands.

"Oh, no," thought Mum "What have I got myself into?" She tried to act as if there was nothing wrong. "I'm here to get Chrissie some religion," Mum the church-goer told herself, not realizing that she was just as lost, as doomed, as the sister-in-law sitting beside her.

When Herbert Harrison stood up to preach, Mum's suspicions were even greater. "Oh, no," She thought, "This isn't a real minister. Where are his robes, where is his clerical collar? Why is he preaching in a normal tone of voice? Why is he so young?" Her eyes fell on the bright, paisley-print tie which Herbert Harrison wore, and she wondered what her vicar would say if he could only see her now!

Worse still, the preacher declared, "Praise the Lord!" In shock, and unable to believe her eyes or her ears, she was convinced she had made a terrible mistake.

Harrison announced his text and began to speak. Mum heard little of what he said, until he declared, "Thou fool, this night thy soul shall be required of thee" (Luke 12:20). That statement was like an arrow that pierced her soul. *"For what is a man profited, if he shall gain the whole world and lose his own soul?"* (Matthew 16:26). Suddenly her anointed moment was coming to be.

Her attention was riveted on the young preacher. Her mouth was dry, and her heart pounded within her. She ceased to be aware of Chrissie seated beside her, or of anyone else nearby. The spotlight of God was shining on her. She felt uncomfortable and unclean. What did she have to do to get rid of her sin? Harrison's words were drifting in and out of her consciousness. One minute she heard his voice, the next her own thoughts. She heard him for a moment: "Confess your sin, and God is faithful and just to forgive." The preacher was pulling in Salvation's net.

"Confess?" Mum began to worry. "Confess? I will never remember all the things I have done wrong."

Suddenly the self-righteous, religious girl began to sense her own need of help. "I'll just tell them the big sins," Mum thought, as she raised her hand in answer to the preacher's appeal. "When I remember the small ones, then I will confess those to him as well."

Harrison asked those who raised their hands to come to the front of the room. Mum stood, and as she did, she was categorizing her sins from "bad" to "not so bad," in preparation to confess! She had become so engrossed in her own anointed moment that she did not see Chrissie come forward as well.

The Camerons were coming to Jesus!

Mum began to confess her sins to the preacher, but he interrupted her: "No, no sister. You don't have to confess to me. Tell Jesus!" Mum took her eyes off the man and turned them toward Jesus. She began to ask Jesus Christ to make her clean, and just as the preacher had said, she felt her burden of sin roll away ~ she was born again! A dance hall would no longer be her only Heaven, and best of all, she knew she would see her baby again. Hope that had once been futile now became an eternal assurance.

A lifetime of dead, unreal religion hadn't done as much for Wendy as two hours of reality. Ornate buildings with stained glass windows had failed, but the Lord Jesus Christ had made all the difference. As Chrissie and Mum walked home that night, their hearts burned within them with excitement and joy.

Mum arrived back at the little shack, took off her hat and coat, and lay down in the bed. She began to think of the great change that knowing Jesus would make, and then she thought about her husband, Simon. Ever since they had met, they had done everything together.

Mum sat bolt upright in bed. "Simon will be so pleased," she thought. "He is going to have a brand-new wife." She reached for the writing paper that was their only contact across the miles between Peterhead and Trieste. As pen touched paper, the joy of what had happened began to pour out.

"My darling Simon, I have great news... I have fallen in love with Jesus. I am going to be a different person when you come home." Mum was so excited at the thought of her soldier husband knowing about Jesus. Jesus was the hope they needed for the start of a new and better life.

She waited anxiously for his response. During those days, her spirits soared, and she imagined the two of them praying together, serving God together, and watching as Jesus made something beautiful of their lives. The Bible became her constant companion, and she spent every spare moment studying God's word and His promises.

Stop Before You Go Too Far

The Italian stamp "Trieste" postmark told her that her wait was over. Her answer had come. Once again, her mind raced to the future, excited at the prospect of good news from Dad. She raced through her uncle's house and into the garden shed that was now her home. She sat down, took a deep breath, and carefully opened the letter.

"Dear Wendy,"

Her stomach tightened into a knot. This salutation was not how Simon began his letters.

"I have just received your letter explaining what you have done. I will not allow my wife to get involved with all this religious nonsense." Mum could hardly believe her eyes! "I am telling you now, stop before you go too far. I will give you 'gloriously saved' when I come home!"

Her cheeks flushed; she found it hard to breathe. *This wasn't her Simon!* It didn't seem like him at all. In a very real sense, it wasn't. He had tasted the sins of the world, and it seemed that nothing could satiate his thirst. The last thing in the world he wanted was a "saved wife."

Her fingers trembled as she folded the letter and placed it back in the envelope. She felt torn, pulled in two directions, between her love for Jesus and her love for Simon.

"I'm saved," she thought. "The preacher said I'd been born again." She recalled Dad's words – "Stop before you go too far." Dad's presence was almost tangible in the small room.

"I've been born again," Mum declared, aloud. "You can't be unborn once you've been born." Her determined voice reflected the momentous decision she was making. "I'm going on. I can't stop serving Jesus. I'm going to pray for Simon to be saved. No matter what, I am going to be faithful."

As with her brother-in-law Michael before her, the young woman did not realize what lay ahead, but she was determined to live for God. Dad was to be in Italy for eighteen more months. Suddenly, the hours that had dragged seemed to fly by. She studied and prayed as if her life depended on it. Dad's stance did not change, and Mum knew that confrontation was inevitable. As each day passed, both fear and excitement grew in her heart. She desperately wanted to see her Simon again, but she was terribly afraid of what would happen when he came home.

The day finally came when Dad was demobilized from the army, and the young soldier returned to Peterhead. The immediate difficulties were enormous and daunting. The man who had returned from Italy was nothing like the person who had left. Mum felt that she was married to a stranger. The young man whom she had married, with whom she had laughed and played was gone. In his place returned a vile and unfeeling person, with whom she had nothing in common.

Setting aside his former gentleness, Dad was determined to show Mum that he was the boss. He intended to turn the threats of his letters into reality. Every day Mum prayed, asking God to show her how to love him.

Dad was hell bent on having his way. The first thing to go was her Bible – he destroyed it and refused to let her to have another. He also prevented her from attending church for three and a half years. Mum was seldom allowed to attend a service. She did manage to find fellowship with other Christians. When shopping, she would meet with other sisters in the Lord, and over a cup of tea, they would pray together. In this way, Mum found an invaluable source of encouragement.

On many occasions, Dad would decide to go to a movie or dance. In Scotland, in those days Christians would never attend such activities. Mum refused to go, but Dad would physically force her to accompany him. In the movie theater, if Mum would not look at the screen, he would beat her.

When things would get very bad, many people, even including some of the Christian women with whom she met, would advise Mum to "get out" before something serious happened. But Mum would reply, "You don't understand. Simon is my husband; we are one flesh. I am going to walk in Heaven with him one day." She knew that Michael had received the answers to his prayers, and she simply believed that God would do the same for her. But at home, things only became worse. Simon was becoming more and more belligerent every day.

Despite all the bad news, there were some bright spots, such as the day when Mum felt something stir within her and recognized that feeling. Her visit to the doctor confirmed what she already knew.

Several months later, a baby girl was born. They called her Wendy. My mother could not have known just how much this little bundle would mean to her in the days ahead. At times, the baby seemed to be the only point of happiness in a life that was becoming more and more miserable.

The living conditions were still very poor. When Wendy was only a few months old, she woke in her tiny cot in the little wooden hut and began to cry. In the half darkness, Mum could see her bottle lying near her face, but when she switched on the light, they discovered a large rat on top of her. It had eaten through the nipple of her bottle, and the milk splashing on her tiny face had caused the baby to wake up.

Mum noticed that Dad's drinking, and all that accompanied his sinful life, had robbed him of any desire for self-advancement. He didn't care to improve his lot in life, or that of his family. He was bound, and he was blind to any chance of a brighter future.

Before the birth of their first child, Mum had entertained many dreams. Everything was going to be perfect – but those dreams had vanished like smoke when Simon Alan died. Now, with Wendy, there was only one thing that counted to Mum: "My daughter will know and love Jesus." Even before she was born, Mum had sung songs about Jesus and had told the child in her womb about Jesus' love. Based on that love, a special closeness grew between mother and daughter. As the wee girl grew, her mother told her stories of Heaven. When Wendy was only three years old, she said to her mom, "I want to ask Jesus into my heart." That transaction was for real and has lasted all her life. My sister Wendy has been one of the mainstays of our family in our quest to serve God.

Several months before that precious moment when Wendy prayed with her, Mum had once again sensed the beginning of life within her. Once again, she was right – I was on my way.

My father worked with his brothers in a business he and Mum had started days after Wendy's birth. They sold nets to farmers and gardeners to cover newly sewn seed. Dad lived a Jekyll and Hyde existence. During the day, he was the hardworking youngest brother and son of the family, but at night, and when alone, he was a degenerate husband and father. In those critical days, my mother clung to the hope that, somehow, God would make a way. But now, there seemed to be no way.

Her pregnancy, as she carried me, was difficult. At one of her visits to the doctor, her worst fear was realized. The doctor could detect no heartbeat. He gave her devastating news: "Your baby will be stillborn. We will make an appointment for you next week to take the baby away." For the second time in her life, she faced the horror of losing her baby.

She lay in bed that night, begging a God she now knew, "Please, not again." Simon's hand happened to be on her stomach as she prayed. "Wendy, did you feel that?" My mum was startled by his voice. "Wendy! That's it again!"

I wasn't dead, as the doctor had said, I was very much alive. Had I not kicked or moved that night, my fate would have been quite different.

Like my brother before me, my birth was very difficult. After 42 hours of labor, and the aid of her brilliant doctor, I was born ~ rather squashed, but alive.

My birth had no impact on my father's life. Nothing changed, as one day blurred into the next. The Cameron family knew only hopelessness and recurring crisis. Mother began to wonder if Dad would ever be saved. She had prayed for seven years, and the dreams of their youth had long since vanished.

She became desperate, and one day, while Dad was at work, she knelt before God in prayer; "Oh, God, I don't know if I even like him anymore. Please give me the grace to stay with him one more month." Her prayers seemed to have the effect of a gas pedal, speeding up the already degenerating situation - Dad got even worse. But she did not stop praying.

The little hut had a sink and a drain that took the water out, but no faucet. Water had to be carried in and heated in a kettle. Often, in the wee hours of the morning, when my Dad hadn't come home, Mum would be washing my diapers and putting them through the old hand wringer that was attached to the sink. Weary and discouraged, she would stop in the middle of her task, lean her head on the ringer, and weep, praying, "Jesus, wherever Simon is, keep him safe. Bring him home to me. Give me grace; please give me the grace to live with him for just one more month."

But Dad just kept getting worse. Mother wondered how she was going to remain strong in her faith, not realizing that underneath and all around her were the everlasting arms of Jesus.

Mum would often speak to little Wendy, and somehow, she seemed to understand the hurt that her mother was feeling. On the long nights when Dad was out, Wendy would be my mum's little friend and confidant. Many times, when my mother was on the verge of giving up, her little girl would come up to her and say, "Mummy, can you please tell me about Heaven?" Mum would lift Wendy up in her lap, look into her brown eyes, hold her close and say, "Oh yes, I'll tell you about Heaven." Then she would describe the golden streets and the gates of pearl. She would talk about the beauty of Jesus, and the end of tears and trials. As she spoke, waves of glory would begin to flow in my mother's heart, and after she tucked the wee lassie into bed, and kissed her on the cheek, she would go back to the washing. With renewed strength, she would say to herself, "Well, I'll try again, I'll pray some more."

Because of the alcohol, darkness, and sin, the Simon that she now lived with was totally different from the Simon she had married. Once, it had been a soft-hearted, likable young boy who respected her and treated her with a love that was sometimes close to worship. Now, he was a hardened drunk who abused and mistreated her.

Many times, he would come home drunk around four o'clock in the morning. The amazing thing is, in those early morning hours, when most wives would have told their husbands to get lost. My Mum would have something for him to eat. Often, he would be too drunk even to get ready for bed, but she would undress him and put him into bed. She would quietly pray over him, but he was so full of hatred he would curse at her, and blame her Jesus for the mess that their marriage was in.

Eventually, her secret prayer was not for enough strength to last a month, but just enough to last a week: "God help me to live with him for one more week." The more she prayed, the worse he got. Wendy didn't realize it, but God was closing the net onto Simon Cameron. Many times, when we ask God to do something, we expect Him to do it our way. But God has His way of working things out according to His pattern and will.

Chapter Four

The Miracle Happens

—✠—

It was Thursday, just another Thursday. Another day of arguments, another day of separation, each one was walking in their own path. My dad came home for lunch. Something was said, and he blew his top. He ranted and raved and walked about cursing at Mum. As he left, he roared, "I hate you, and I hate your Jesus!" He proceeded to yell that he didn't like the children all that much either and that he was sick of their marriage. He'd had it! "I'll never come back. I don't want to see your face again," he shouted, slamming the door behind him.

Mum had prayed for seven years. She had put up with abuse, and she had put up with long nights alone. Her only comfort to help her had been her little daughter's questions about Heaven. Now, she stood holding her little girl with one hand, and me, a baby in my cot. She had no idea of what to do and such a sense of failure swept through her being.

Worn and tired, she began to weep. She had never thought she would say these words, but finally, in despair, she said, "I can't stand him anymore." She cried out in prayer, "God, I can't take it. I'm going to give him to you." At that exact time, Dad was back at his work. He was now working at a wood factory with his brothers. They had expanded their business from making nets to manufacturing wooden buildings. Working with a 30-inch wood saw, he looked at the sawdust covered clock. It was 3:00 pm. He didn't know what was about to happen. Neither did Mum. But God was about to do the unexpected.

Dad looked down at the wooden plank in his hands, trying to concentrate on the end that was approaching the whirling blade. Suddenly, something came over him. He didn't feel right. He shook himself and tried to shut off this strange feeling. "What's wrong with me?" he thought. He tried to regain his composure. To his amazement, he started to tremble. Tears began to stream down his face.

He had heard his brother Michael pray for seven years, "God save my brother Simon." He had watched his wife pray faithfully and live a godly life before him for seven more years. It had taken fourteen years for Simon Cameron to come to this point.

He looked at the blurred saw and the wood again. His hands were trembling. Then he realized that his legs, his knees, in fact, his whole body was shaking! The tears began to flow as if his heart would break. The dam had burst.

One of his brothers walked past and saw him standing there, transfixed to the spot. He was shaking and trying to fight back tears that nothing could stop. "What's wrong with you, Simon?"

In his Scottish dialect, Simon said, "I dinna ken." ~ "I don't know."

"You'd better get away from that saw, or you'll cut your hands off," John replied. "Come up to the office with me," his brother said. Like a sheep being led, Dad went up, and they sat him down on an old small sofa. His mother was there, and she made him a cup of strong tea. She knelt and looked into her boy's face. She had seen him at crisis points before in his life, but this was different.

"Simon," she pleaded, "what's wrong with you?"

Once again, fighting through the tears and the shaking and the river of emotion, he said, "I dinna ken." "I dinna ken."

Then she suggested, "The best thing we can do is take him home to Wendy!"

They helped him into the car where he lay down on the back seat. There was no comforting him. They couldn't talk to him; they couldn't reason with him. They eventually decided that he was having a nervous breakdown.

They carried him home, knocked on the door and Mum opened it. She had every right in the world to turn him away and say, "I don't want him near me ever again. I've suffered enough. He has caused me enough grief, and I don't want to see him anymore."

She had prayed seven years for this moment, but when she saw him, she didn't understand what was taking place.

She let them in and helped Dad to a chair. His brothers explained what had happened, and then left her alone with her husband. Little Wendy was playing outside, and I was still a baby in my crib, just a year old.

My mother looked at him and said, "Simon, what's wrong?"

He could only repeat, "I dinna ken." "I dinna ken!" And then the Spirit of God began to move in her heart. "Simon, I think God is dealing with you," she paused. "I think it's the conviction of the Holy Ghost." He looked at her, incredulously. But instead of the usual violence, silence met her. She picked up more courage.

"Simon, the Holy Ghost has a hold of you."

Once again, his tears flowed. He was too broken to speak.

Then Mum said, Simon, "The Bible says that if you call upon the name of the Lord, you shall be saved."

Up to this point, Dad had had nothing to do with the Bible. Prayer was revolting to him. He had totally rejected God and was proud of it.

But Mum said, "Call upon the Lord," and he took it that she meant he had to shout. Through his tears, he lifted his hands and looked heavenward. Through the poverty and drunkenness, through all the days and years of bondage that he had known, a hungry heart cried out to God.

"Jesus tak' me." He spoke in his Scottish dialect; Jesus is the greatest linguist that man has ever known. Right there and then, a drunk, vile sinner who most people wouldn't dream of visiting, opened his heart, and the King of Glory walked in.

Dad always said he could still remember when the first wave of God's forgiveness hit him. I have good news for you, reader: God has an ocean of forgiveness, and not many days from now, the anointed moment is coming for your loved ones.

Mum had waited seven years for this anointed moment. Dad had passed from death unto life. It was a surprise, to say the least.

Now Mum realized that the closer he had come to the moment of salvation, the harder he had become. So many times, people have given up praying and believing, when they might be one prayer away from breaking Heaven's power over their loved one. I know it can be difficult, but the promise is to the overcomer!

Sometimes, God will take people kicking and screaming into the Kingdom of God. That's how it was with Simon Cameron. That day, he poured out his heart to God. He couldn't stop weeping for three days and three nights—all-day Friday, Saturday and Sunday.

He wept himself completely out of his sin and into fellowship with God through Jesus Christ.

He often said that when he opened his eyes after asking Jesus to take him, the lights seemed to be turned on with double-power electricity. The greens were greener, the blues were bluer, and the reds were redder. Suddenly the burden of his sin had been taken away.

Let me say this – Simon Cameron would never have been saved if someone had said, "Oh, it doesn't matter about sin. God will forgive and just forget about it." Dad knew that his sins needed paying for. It was a bleeding, dying, butchered Savior, hanging on Calvary for his personal sins that finally broke him. It wasn't damnation preaching. It wasn't the threat of Hell or eternal darkness, but it was the Love of God that brought him to repentance. It wholly overwhelmed him.

When Dad had been in the world, he was totally consumed by the pleasures of sin. He said that when he came to Christ, God did not take away the drive or the "want-to" from his life. The Lord just converted it! Simon Cameron came into the Kingdom at ten thousand miles an hour and continued to do so until he went to be with his lovely Savior.

As he was motivated by God to do great things for Him, Mum had finally seen her prayers answered. In the morning times when they woke, she would glance over to see her sleeping husband, and in his first instants of consciousness, his hands would lift toward Heaven. Tears would stream down his face, and a torrent of thanksgiving would flow from his lips towards God for his wonderful salvation.

On the Monday morning after his conversion, Dad got up to go to work. As he left the house, he noticed for the first time that the street which he had walked down every day was lined with trees. The air was cleaner. Everything was more wonderful. The words of an old hymn express the wonder of the experience his heart was now singing about. "Heaven above, a softer blue, Earth beneath a fairer green. Something lives in every hue, Christless eyes have never seen."

As Simon Cameron walked that day, he was still, in material terms, in poverty, but the difference was this – he was changed from the inside! It seemed that the birds in the trees were singing that Simon Cameron had been reconciled to God. From that day on, the world wasn't just improved; it was completely different.

His hunger for God was insatiable. On one occasion, one of the elders of a church came to the new convert and said, "Simon, I know you're excited just now, but it will soon wear off, and you will return to normal." What foolishness! Surely every day with Jesus is sweeter than the day before! The excitement never did wear off! The last moments I was with him was in a hospital in Aberdeen, Scotland. I had flown home all night, having heard of his medical crisis. I rushed from the airport and made it to his room. I walked in, gave him a hug and asked him how he was. His first words were, "Will you be home this weekend? I want to hear my son preach?" And, as the machines whirred around him, he took my hand and looked deep inside me, "What are we doing for Jesus? Tell me about Moldova."

I never heard him say no to God. He jumped off cliffs of faith without a thought. He was reckless in everything he did regarding Heaven. One day he came in to the wooden hut. He hadn't been saved for very long. There was a single bed, a drop-leaf table, two small stools, a tiny wardrobe, a small chair and a sink with no faucets. They had two soup bowls, two knives, two forks and two spoons that were used for every meal they had. In other words, they had next to nothing. "Wendy," Dad looked at her with complete earnestness.

"How little can we live on? I've just read in the Bible where they came and laid their possessions at the Apostle's feet. What can we give away?" Wendy looked around their tiny world and couldn't think of a thing they could afford to lose. Her newly saved husband remained as reckless in his love for God until the day he died.

The Miracles Continue

The doctor who had shown such great skill in saving both my mother and me during my birth had a problem which besets many folks, especially, it seems the Scots. He and his wife shared the same "family curse."

Scotland makes money by producing the world's Scotch whiskey, but pays a horrific price for it. Statistics indicate that one in four people who are in mental hospitals in Scotland are there because of alcohol.

My mother always felt grateful to the doctor for her babies, and one day she noticed him in town, looking rather down at the heel. For no reason, other than gratitude and a desire to show Christian kindness, my mother began going down to help in the doctor's home. The doctor and his wife's alcohol problems had brought them much hardship. The doctor's house had, in fact, belonged to his mother-in-law, who had bought it to establish him in his medical practice.

Mum would clean the house, get the children ready for school and wash their clothes. Then she would prepare the doctor's examination room where the practice took place. The place she had sat in years before learning of the existence of Simon Alan Cameron. With Dad's encouragement, she did all she could to help this family that was being robbed of so much by their alcoholism.

Eventually, everything fell to pieces for the doctor. When his practice collapsed, it was found that he had not been able to pay the mortgage for over a year, and so, the house reverted to his mother-in-law. She advertised the house in the newspaper, and there were many prospective buyers interested in the property.

One day, my mother met my father after work. With that familiar smile and look ~ "Don't ask any questions, just follow." She said, "Simon, I've got the key to our doctor's old house. It's for sale, and we're going down to look at it."

The young man who was making less than twenty dollars a week looked at his wife and said, "Wendy you've got to be kidding. You are joking, aren't you? We don't have enough money to buy the front door handle!"

With that, his red-headed wife smiled and said, "Well, a cat can look at a queen."

They went into the house. My mother knew it well, for she had spent much time there. She showed my father around every nook and cranny ~ there were thirteen rooms in it. Of course, the house was perfect, all and more than they had ever dreamed a house could be.

But all the time Dad was thinking, "This wife of mine is crazy."

The next day, my mother returned the key to the attorney who was responsible for the sale of the house, and said, "The house is beautiful."

That afternoon the owner went down to the attorney's office and considered the offers that had been made. There were some very handsome offers, and she provisionally decided which to accept. The lawyer casually said, "Simon and Wendy Cameron were in and they looked at the house yesterday."

"Simon and Wendy Cameron?" She asked, as she stopped in her tracks. The lawyer, questioning himself, looked back at his documents. "Yes, Simon and Wendy Cameron."

"Send for them," she insisted.

Wooden huts don't have phones, but somehow, the lawyer tracked them down. They left my sister and me with Aunt Yolande and Uncle Lionel and got dressed in the finest clothes they could find. Dad borrowed a car and drove out to the country to see the owner in her very grand home.

My father looked at the floor and saw wall-to-wall carpeting for the first time in his life. The fleeting thought passed through his mind that, if he fell, he would never be found again in the thick, luxurious pile of the carpet.

She led them into her elegant living room, and they sat down on the fine furniture. They were served tea and biscuits. Then the owner fixed her gaze on the young couple and said, "I hear you have been down looking at my house." Dad's eyes glanced at hers for a moment and then fell instantly to the floor, embarrassed because he felt he was only wasting this wealthy and important lady's time.

Mum spoke up, "Yes we have, and we loved it. We thought it was beautiful." The lady spoke to Dad again, "Simon, are you interested in buying the house?"

My Dad looked at Mum and then went over to the lady, and answered, "Well, yes, we would like to buy it."

She said, "How much could you afford to give me for the house?" At this point, even my Mum wanted to run away.

My father's tongue stuck in his now dry mouth. He was convinced that the next words he spoke were going to be met with a torrent of abuse and insults for such folly, and an invitation to leave. He looked at Mum, then did some calculations of the dreams in his mind, and said, "Your house is perfect." (It was four and one-half stories high, had thirteen rooms, eighteen-inch granite walls, and two-inch solid wood floors. The house was a beautiful mansion that had been built for a steamer captain). It seemed an eternity as he glanced from Mum again to the lady ~ then to Mum and back to the lady. Both waited for some profound statement to come from his lips.

"Well," he coughed, trying to clear his throat. "Well," as he tried to speak again, a tight feeling came into his chest, Simon looked down at the floor again, thinking, "I can't tell her the situation, she'll be so annoyed."

"It's all right," she said. "Tell me what you can afford to pay for the house."

"The fact is," said Dad, "the most I can afford," his dry tongue tried to form words, "is eight hundred pounds." That is worth about twelve hundred dollars today.

With that, Mum nearly fell out of the chair. Eight hundred pounds! She had never seen that much money! He continued, "And furthermore (he was finding new strength in the fact that she hadn't passed out at his first statement), we would need you to co-sign for us to get a loan."

She looked at Mum and then back to Dad, slowly repeating, "Eight hundred pounds, is that the most you can offer?"

Dad thought, "I knew it. This is crazy. Wendy should never have talked me into this."

She stood up, and Dad felt he was about to be escorted out of her house.

She fumbled in her pocket, took out a key and said, "Wendy, you have been kind and good to my daughter and my son-in-law. I know about the mornings that you helped get their family ready for school. You've shown a fine example of how a Christian should be."

Stretching her hand out with the key toward Mum, she said, "Wendy, because of your kindness to my daughter and my son-in-law, the house is yours." She passed the key into Mum's hand. She continued, "My lawyer will think I'm crazy, but I don't care. The house was meant for you. Congratulations."

They left her house that evening so excited. Nothing would do except to go down to have another look at it in the evening light. They dedicated the house to the Lord that night. In the years that followed, many people would come to stay there, and many souls came to Christ in that house.

By no means is this the whole story of the Camerons. That would take another book. It is simply the testimony of what God can do for a family. Somehow, in mercy and love, God reached down, looked beyond our faults, and saw our need.

God can use you where you are. First, God used Michael, then Yolande, two young evangelists and finally, my mother. Because of this, I am saved today.

The Bible says, *"Lo, children are a heritage of the Lord"* (Psalm 127:3). It also states, speaking of a virtuous woman, that *"her children arise up, and call her blessed"* (Proverbs 31:28).

Whatever heights my ministry may attain, whatever success any of our family may achieve in this life, we owe it first to God and second to a young girl who decided to follow Jesus, and who would not be denied! She had lost her baby and had endured poverty, physical abuse, and treatment that would make most people turn their backs in bitterness against God.

Through all of this, one young girl held on to God's promise of Household Salvation. She received the promise. Now, it's time for you to move forward and claim Household Salvation.

Part II

Chapter Five

The Reality of Hell

—ɯ—

I sat at my desk in the middle of a hectic day. I paused from writing an article and, for just a moment, turned my heart toward God. I knew he had been trying to speak to me. I know you have had that feeling before, too. I just had not been listening.

The phone rang, interrupting my thoughts. It was a good friend of mine, so I felt obligated to take the call. After some pleasantries, she said, "Do you know that 7,000 people die every hour and 6,000 of them end up in hell?" As she finished this devastating statement, her other phone rang. "I've got to go." With that, she hung up.

As I put down the phone, my mind returned to the disquiet I had been feeling. On the outward, things couldn't be better. We were on nation-wide television, and our ministry was growing. Things I could only dream about were coming true. But I knew God was trying to get through to my spirit. I half-whispered in desperate earnest, "I wish I knew what You are trying to tell me."

My request, felt like I had thrown a switch. "I'll show you."

Sitting back in my chair, I immediately felt the strong presence of God. Until this time, I had never received a vision from God. In fact, I have always been rather skeptical of such manifestations, and have viewed them warily.

I closed my eyes. Suddenly I saw what I could only describe as a massive conveyor belt on which stood all mankind. I was there, so were you. We were laughing, playing, working and in general, just living life. There were tiny newborn babies joining our relentless journey. To my amazement, no one seemed to notice the direction in which we were going.

I began to be concerned about where this moving platform was taking us. Suddenly, I saw the end of the journey. It was horrific. Thousands of people were one minute living a normal life, and then the next minute they fell off the edge into an inferno! Their screams and cries were muffled by the roar of the flames that engulfed them. I tried to tell those around me, but the noise of life had made them deaf to my desperate pleas.

I began to sob, and then, beyond sobbing, to travail! Suddenly, Hell wasn't a distant place that no one speaks of. It was an imminent event, claiming what seemed an innumerable number of people who would never see the light of day again.

I was sick and scared. I didn't want to see any more. This was not the side of eternity that I wanted to experience.

I was experiencing real, physical pain at the thought of what I had just seen. I was upset, first at what I had witnessed, and secondly at God for making me feel so uncomfortable.

From that vision, God took me back to riding in the car with my brother Neil, an event which had occurred only two weeks prior. My "step-grandmother" had died in my mother's arms, as my mother begged her to give her heart to Jesus. She refused, cursing until her last breath. I missed her funeral by a few days. My brother and I had gone down to the local fish and chip shop for some supper. Even though I was sitting at my desk, spiritually I was back in the car and could feel the warmth of the hot food on my lap. BBC news was on the radio. The wiper blades swished back and fore on the windscreen.

"In there," pointed Neil. "She is buried over there, beside the new wall." I could see the flowers on her grave, still fresh. The sadness that I felt when I first heard the news of her death swept over me again.

Then, God spoke. "She is not in that graveyard," I heard Him say to me. "She will never laugh again, never know peace again. She is lost. She is one of the ones you saw falling into Hell."

I did not think I could stand much more of this dealing with God, but He continued, "When you are fifty, she will still be in Hell. When you are seventy, she will still be in hell. When you have been in Heaven for ten thousand years, she will still be in Hell." I felt physically sick. I'd had enough.

"There is no parole from Hell." His words were lethal. "Once lost, once past grace, there is no mercy." My eyes were burning with tears.

During God's dealings with me, my father had called and heard my wails of agony. He and my mother stayed up all night to pray for me in their home in Scotland. Mother prayed that night, "Whatever you are doing with Philip Lord, may his pain be for a reason, and Your glory."

In just a few hours I had come from wondering why I hadn't seen what I felt should have been the response to my ministry, to know without a shadow of a doubt what was wrong. God had to show me Hell and my loved ones falling over the edge of time, to convince me of the need for Household Salvation. He communed with me again. "Son, most of my Church has lost the urgency to win the lost. That urgency comes from the realization of eternal Hell. My love has been preached, my provision has been taught, but my justice had been neglected."

I thought shamefully of how long it had been since I had last spoken of Hell. I, too, was guilty of the sin of omission. That afternoon changed my life forever.

To remove God's judgment from the picture dilutes grace, and redemption to mere conveniences, rather than to man's most important need.

God's grace would not be needed if there was no such thing as the judgment bar. As the Church faces the greatest test of its existence, preachers are proclaiming the goodness of God and are totally neglecting the severity of God. His goodness was the ark; his severity was the flood. His goodness was shown as the angels warned Lot; His severity was shown in the pillar of salt.

Unless we realize the necessity for Salvation, that an unsaved soul, no matter how much that soul is loved by you or me will be destined to eternal damnation, we will not be compelled by the Holy Ghost to see them come to Christ.

Instead of silly arguments and banter between the redeemed and the damned, the realization of impending Hell gives force and power to the believer, who may otherwise be hindered by timidity or pride.

It is the scream of the emergency siren in all its severity that causes our heart to race, as we steer clear of its desperate rush. We know that someone is in trouble, and for an instant, we too become part of the passing emergency. When one is gripped with approaching Hell, the present becomes precious! TODAY is the day of salvation!

I know this is a terrifying thought, but I must tell you ~ your husband or wife, son or daughter, mother or father, brother or sister, uncle, aunt, cousin or grandchild is going to be in Hell unless he or she is saved. Your loved one will fall into a place of total isolation, of outer darkness, where there is weeping and wailing and gnashing of teeth. It is a region of eternal torture, where nothing and no one can help; the land of the damned cut off from God and you forever. What do you intend to do about telling them of salvation?

"Soon will the season of rescue be o'er... Soon will they drift to eternity's shore."

We have gone from giving little thought to Earthly comforts, only preparing for Heaven and the sweet by and by, until today when many preachers deal only with the comforts of the sweet here and now. We have gone from one extreme to the other. It was once thought to almost be a sin to consider oneself as worthy through Jesus' blood. As a boy, I remember being told just how wretched and unworthy a man was. It crippled any sense of sonship and awareness of the joy our Heavenly Father had in us. All that mattered was, "some golden daybreak." For years, the Church was beset by such thought.

Today the pendulum has swung to the other extreme. It seems that today's "seeker-friendly, hyper-grace" movement has turned Christ's church into a club. We have made God in our image, rather than being made in His. How little we hear of the Gospel appeal to the sin-burdened heart. I feel that it's time to get things back to the middle ground. Yes, I believe God gives grace, but I also know we must keep our eyes on eternity. I would rather die well, in the knowledge of Household Salvation, than live well a selfish life that would lead to an impoverished death. Instead of, "What must I do to be saved?" the question has become, "What must I do be blessed?" The line has been smudged, and conviction is old-fashioned. The Blood is rarely, if ever mentioned. We have become fixated on presentation, and we seem to forget that before there were smoke machines and intelligent lighting, the Gospel worked in the open fields with a tree stump as a pulpit.

Time Is Running Out

After this time of dealing with God, everything changed. My vision changed, my desire changed. Even the Bible changed. I couldn't open the Book without finding the thread of redemption through families, from Genesis, Exodus throughout the whole Bible. I wanted to know, not only about Hell itself, but how best to express to my brothers and sisters in Christ, exactly how desperate the situation is.

My search began in the following verse from Chapter 16 of Luke's Gospel:

"There was a certain rich man, which was clothed in purple and fine linen, and fared sumptuously every day: And there was a certain beggar named Lazarus, which was laid at his gate, full of sores, and desiring to be fed with the crumbs which fell from the rich man's table: moreover the dogs came and licked his sores. And it came to pass that the beggar died, and was carried by the angels into Abraham's bosom: the rich man also died, and was buried; And in Hell he lifted up his eyes, being in torments, and seeth Abraham afar off, and Lazarus in his bosom. And he cried and said, Father Abraham, have mercy on me, and send Lazarus that he may dip the tip of his finger in water, and cool my tongue; for I am tormented in this flame. But Abraham said, Son, remember that thou in thy lifetime receivest thy good things, and likewise Lazarus evil things: but now he is comforted, and thou art tormented. And beside all this, between us and you there is a great gulf fixed: so that they which would pass from hence to you cannot: neither can they pass to us that would come from thence. Then he said, I

pray thee therefore, Father, that thou wouldest send him to my Father's house:

For I have five brethren: that he may testify unto them, lest they also come into this place of torment. Abraham saith unto him, they have Moses and the prophets; let them hear them. And he said, Nay, Father Abraham but if one went unto them from the dead, they will repent. And he said unto him, "If they hear not Moses and the prophets, neither will they be persuaded, though one rose from the dead." (Luke 16:19-31).

What a graphic picture of the agony of eternal torment! Here is an amazing story full of color and complexity. A rich man, a beggar, dogs, sores, and death. As the fine silk of his garments brushed against his skin, the rich man gave little or no thought to eternity. A few feet away, covered in sores and surviving on crumbs was a man called Lazarus. It is interesting, isn't it? We know the beggar's name, yet the rich man is nameless forever? They both die within a short space of time. Stark, unpoetic language marked the rich man's demise. Whereas, the angels swept Lazarus into Abraham's bosom. Here's something we don't think about: Lazarus is in Heaven, the rich man is in Hell, and they can still see each other. Could it be that the torment of Hell is a consciousness of Heaven that can never be attained? Not only could he see Lazarus, but was able to identify Abraham, and the next words are stunning, "Father Abraham." He was no pagan, no heathen unaware of God or His covenant. This man recognized Abraham. The arrogance of wealth did not die with his body. He commanded the beggar to come and cool his tongue.

The devastation of realization that between them was "a great gulf fixed" – a great divide. Then the last recorded words from Hell are heard, "Please, send him to warn my five brothers lest they too come to this place of torment." He wasn't giving last minute instruction on how he wanted his will settled, or his unfinished business, which death had interrupted, to be finished. *Household Salvation was the thing that was screamed across the great divide.*

Eternity is coming! We will escape Hell if we have trusted in the saving power of Christ; but what of our loved ones? What provision are we making for them to join us?

Some people have simply never thought about it. Others just don't care. We MUST care! We MUST pray!

We MUST reach them now! We cannot afford to spare any effort if we are to win our families to Christ.

Romans 6:23 is a well-known verse which tells us that, "the wages of sin is death." That "great gulf" we have just read about is what makes Hell such a tragic fate. For those in Hell will be separated from a loving, caring, God, who is the source of all life and goodness. Hell is death; it is irreversible separation from He who is life. For all eternity multitudes will know nothing of love, compassion, gentleness, comfort or any of those things that are so vital to life, but as mentioned before may be witness to such things, as the rich man was. Such misery is almost too great to think about.

We live today in a world of equivocation. What only a few years ago was unthinkable is now not only accepted but promoted. The term, "you don't know me" with a puffed-up chest and a pointed finger and a chin stuck out in rebellion have become the defense for a generation. The Church doesn't talk. It sits silently, as if we are no longer relevant. An opinion poll matters more than God's Word. We are so desperate to be liked that we have lost clarity. What were once commands, are now gentle suggestions; but if they make you feel uncomfortable, it's ok. Stark contrast to the interchange between Lazarus, Abraham, and the rich ruler.

The Church is not a club, a place to come and have coffee and donuts on Sunday morning, hear a great worship band and get a pep talk to make us feel good about ourselves. I like coffee and donuts. I like good music. I love to hear preaching. But unless there are a point and a reason behind it, it loses its point and reason.

When we stand and sing, we are continuing the song of the redeemed. We join the chorus of the stars that serenaded Adam and Eve in the Garden. We are the song of Moses and David and the priests in the temple and the song of the martyr and covenanter. We are a course of blocks in the building that is called the Church. We rest on those that have gone before, whose foundation of the Gospel was clear, unequivocal and relevant. Jesus is coming soon, but if He doesn't come soon, what foundation have we left for our children and grandchildren to come?

I love my grandbabies more than life. I would give them the world. But things will not make their future bright. Faith will. Salvation will. Knowing the power of the Cross is the heritage we must leave.

Your theology may lead you to any one of the various viewpoints of how this world will reach its end ~ but none can deny the fact that there isn't much time left. When the Church is raptured, when we, the salt of the Earth are gone, the final curtain will be almost ready to fall on the stage of human history. There will be some then who, though alive, will already be condemned to the torture of the Hell we have been talking about.

If this is true ~ and it is ~ then time is truly running out for those of our loved ones who are still not saved. It's time to discover the promises of God for you and your house. It's time to claim the unclaimed promise and see God do miracles in your family. It's time for Household Salvation.

I have said much about the reality of Hell because we must realize just how vital it is for us to win our loved ones to Christ, but, if Hell is real, then so is Heaven. Only a fool would not want his or her family to share in the glory and joy of spending eternity in the presence of His Majesty, King Jesus. The promise is yours. IT'S TIME TO CLAIM IT NOW!

Chapter Six

Drive Satan From Your Field

—✺—

I sat once more at my desk, still broken by the vision God had given me. I was haunted by the agony and torment of those multitudes. It had been personalized by the graveyard and the acute sense of personal loss. Each time I thought of my loved ones ~ lost forever, suffering eternal torture with no remedy, no consolation ~ I broke down in uncontrollable fits of weeping. My eyes were red and swollen by the flow of the relentless dam~burst of tears. I closed them and tried to compose myself.

"Lord," I prayed, "Why are you dealing with me like this? What is it you want me to do?"

Immediately, in my spirit, God lead me by the hand as if I was a small boy, to a large green field. In the field were my loved ones. I saw my wife and children, grandchildren, my mother, father, sisters, and brother, as well as other friends and relatives.

"This is your life. It's your field," I heard the Lord say. I looked at it. Everyone was happy. Things seemed well. Mine was a good field, and I could be pleased with all I was seeing. I felt relief to have shifted from the horror of the waterfall and the graveyard.

Out of the corner of my eye, something seemed to stir. I turned around quickly, but no, there was nothing there, only my loved ones happily living out their lives. Still, I began to feel uneasy. Something wasn't right. Then I saw him - crouched in the corner of the field, clutching chains in his hands, barely visible amid so many busy people. With an evil sneer on his face, Satan looked down at my loved ones as they lived, loved, dreamed and sought to fulfill all that God had created them to be. I saw him laughing wickedly to himself. He acted as if he knew he was not permitted to be there, yet was hoping I did not notice him.

I said to Jesus, still holding onto His hand, "Look, Satan is in my field." He looked at me, and said, "Well, it is your field. I have given you the authority over your field."

Then I began to understand something which I need to share with you and the importance of which you need to realize. In my field, I had seen all of those in my sphere of influence. It was my job to sow the seed which would result in the kind of harvest I wanted to reap in my life. Yet, in all my busy working, I had made a critical mistake. I had allowed Satan to enter my field.

The Bible says, "Resist the devil, and he will flee from you" (James 4:7). Many of us have developed the idea that to resist the devil means to spend fifteen minutes now and then praying and binding Satan's efforts. That's good, but sometimes it's only giving him a little push. It might be enough to knock him off balance for a moment, but it is not resisting him – it is not getting him out of your field.

I'm not a small person; I am over six feet tall, and no lightweight. If you want to move me anywhere, you had better apply lots of muscle. If we expect to push Satan out of our field, we had better learn to call on the resources of Heaven. Our walk with God, our commitment to a Spirit-led, Word-governed life, all determine how much resistance we are capable of. The weapons are there. The ammunition is available. We have only to keep the lines of communication open to the Commander-in-Chief to know how to mount the attack.

Fifteen minutes of training now and then does not keep any army fit to repel an enemy. Neither can we expect to deal with the enemy of our souls without a 100 percent commitment to RESISTANCE.

We are blessed in that we know the promise, *"Resist the devil and he will flee."* But resist we must. We must drive him out. The eternal destiny of those we care for most demands that there be no compromise. Many are content to cultivate their field and then, when they bump into the devil, say, "Excuse me," and simply make a detour. No! We must *resist* him; *drive him out* in the name of Jesus and the authority of His Holy Word. We can settle for nothing less than the complete removal of his wicked works from the fields of our lives. What about your field? Will you let him stay or will you relentlessly drive him out?

When we get him out, we must also ensure that he stays out. The devil has no answer to the miracle of salvation. Each one of us who claims Christ as his or her Savior has the means to be free forever from the power of sin. The enemy will make every effort to decimate the influence which our lives have on those we love. For this reason, we cannot afford to let him sneak back into our field. A little gossip here, a little dishonesty there, a moment of compromise and the field where our loved ones are can be once again at his mercy. RESIST HIM.

Here are some thoughts to help you understand that you are not fighting this battle alone.

Your Transferred Authority

When I was a little boy, we had an ironmonger in our town called Bruce's. It was an old-fashioned Home Depot. As I write, I can still smell the strange, but wonderful atmosphere of brooms and nails, paper, and straw. It was a wondrous place of discombobulating where anything would be placed anywhere; paint would be placed next to shovels. I loved going there as a boy with my Dad.

Dad was fixing something in the big house that had become our home. I was old enough now to go places by myself. He called me one day, and very seriously said to me, "Philip, I want you to run an errand for me. I want you to go to Bruce's. Do you think you can manage?" Now, back then, from our house to Bruce's was an expedition: along King Street, down York Street, onto Queen Street, turn right past the Fish and Chip shop, the Kit-Kat Cafe, and just on the bend sat the object of my adventure.

Dad played a trick on me that day that I play on my grandkids to this day "Be quick," He said. "I will be counting."

He wrote what he needed on a piece of brown paper sack, with one of those big carpenter's pencils, and proceeded to count. In about ten minutes, I was standing at the big wooden counter, which was covered in chips and dings from decades of use. The smell of the oil that preserved the nuts and bolts from rust filled the air.

I squared my shoulders and looked up at the gray-haired man, then stuck out my hand and said, "I am Philip Cameron. My dad, Simon, said for me to give you this" and handed him the paper. It was, to date, the most amazing thing I had ever seen. I had no idea until that minute, the power of *transferred authority*. I was a kid. If I had met the same man out on the street and stood before him as I did in that store, he would have cuffed me on the ear and sent me home. But something was different. He took the paper and began to gather the items listed.

Talk about feeling important. In a few minutes, the man handed me the items, wrapped neatly in brown paper and carefully taped closed. He didn't ask for money because Dad had an account. Feeling certain that my dad was now counting in the thousands, I quickly took the packet and ran and feeling very important as I hurried out of Bruce's the Ironmonger.

The importance didn't belong to me: it belonged to my dad. There is a chorus we used to sing in church, *"He signed my deed with His atoning blood, He ever lives to make His promise sure. Though all the hosts of Hell march in to make the second claim, they all march out at the mention of His Name."*

You might have to do the running. You might have to be faithful to get to the "Bruce the Ironmonger" of your life. But trust me, the minute you use His Name, Hell has no answer. The argument is over. To quote my dad, Simon Peter, who said it a thousand times, "When you trust in God, help is already on the way."

From the very beginning of Scripture, we are shown who it is who can keep the devil out of our field. Romans 16:20 tells us, *"And the God of Peace shall bruise Satan under your feet shortly…"* It is God's power that can bruise Satan under our feet. It is not our abilities, or our talents, or anything other than our total dependence on, and commitment to, Him. Jesus, living in us, will bruise

Satan's head and thwart his evil plans for us, and our loved ones.

The last word of Romans 16:20 is "shortly." God wants us to get Satan out of our field immediately! There is no reason, no good one that is for delay. IT'S TIME ~ to lift our foot, bruise Satan's head, and drive him out of our field in the name of Jesus!

Your Transferred Power

World War II was at its most critical time. Germany ruled Europe. Pearl Harbor had brought America out of its neutrality and into the war. The date was June 6, 1944. The weather over the English Channel had been atrocious, but the greatest invading force that had ever been seen, amassed in the twenty or so miles between the white cliffs of Dover and the rocky cliffs of Normandy, France. A force of more than 160,000 Allied troops landed along the 50-mile stretch of the French Coast Line. They were supported by more than 5,000 ships and 13,000 aircraft. The cost of lives on D-Day was horrendous. More than 9,000 allied soldiers were killed or wounded.

I've been there. I've looked up from the beach and down from the cliff, and shuddered at the thought of what these young American, Canadian and British boys faced that day. It wasn't a sure thing. General Dwight D. Eisenhower had, in his pocket, a speech taking responsibility for the full failure of the invasion, in case their attempt was unsuccessful. When the big barge doors lowered, the men surged into the deadly teeth of German machine guns, and many died before their feet got wet in the chilly waters of the English Channel. What seemed like countless hours passed and worse still, countless young boys lost. Nevertheless, a bridgehead was established on the coast of Normandy

The sacrifice paid by those amazing men was reinforced by the might and power of the production of the United States and its ability to produce armaments. Every factory: General Motors, Ford, General Electric and everyone thousands of miles away ~ including the Rosie the Riveter ~ turned out Jeeps, medicine, and ammunition. You name it; they made it. The world's greatest power was focused on a few hundred yards of sandy shore. Within hours, hospitals, oil depots, mechanic shops, cafes, bunkhouses ~ everything imaginable, needed to continue the fight ~ poured into that tiny space on the coast. The power of American military might had turned the logistics of the war.

The moment you got saved, you were God's beachhead into your household. You might not see it, but I can assure you that the battle is not yours, it is the Lord's. If you show up, He will fight the battle. All Heaven's power will focus on piercing the darkness in your family and will cause the light to shine.

Your Transferred Resources

My brother Neil was visiting me and my family in America. I asked the question I have asked so many times, already knowing the answer that was about to come. With only a few days of his vacation left before he returned to Scotland, I asked him, "Is there anything else you would like to see or do?"

His boys were small at the time. He asked in a low tone, "Do you think we could go to Disney World?" His tone wasn't low enough! Within seconds, the news had spread through the house; "We are going to Disney World!"

My son Philip had just celebrated his birthday. He came up with big doe eyes and said, "If you are taking Uncle Neil to Disney World, can we come too?"

So, began an indelible lesson on the realization of the power of *transferred resources.* We drove to Florida, found a hotel, and got to the gates of the Magic Kingdom. Now let me tell you this: As I said before, everyone, it seems, who comes to visit us ends up leading me to the Magic Kingdom, and so it was. We paid our tickets, walked past the big clock and into the first square. Philip had taken all the birthday money he had been given by family and friends, with him. While we were on the tram, he asked me to keep his money safe, which he kept in one of my old wallets. So now, I had two wallets in my pockets.

As we walked through the square, his eyes fell upon the first corner store (many of you probably know the one I am talking about). It is where they cut silhouettes. The doe eyes returned and said, "Dad, can me and Melody get one of these made?"

I stopped him dead in his tracks. "Don't be silly. That's not necessary." Then came the line to end all lines, "It's okay Dad. I will use my money." I just had been completely set up. How could I, a loving father, take my boy's money to buy his silhouette?

Two minutes later, it was a Mickey Mouse hat – for him and Mel. Then, a banana dipped in chocolate and nuts. Throughout the day, those doe eyes *robbed me blind*. I walked forever, my feet screaming complaints after the first fifteen minutes. I thought the day would never come to an end, while this little pirate robbed me at every turn. "It's okay Dad. I will use my money." (By the way, I do mean pirate. He got a swashbuckling sword, too).

At the end of the day, crippled with pain and laden with junk, I made it back to the clock and limped toward the trams that would take me back to the safety of my car. As I stood awaiting our tram, I felt someone try to rob me. I reached around behind me and grabbed a little arm that was attached to...

Doe eyes.

What nerve! What cheek! He opened the wallet in front of me, took out the money and counted it. Then, with a smile that mocked my softness, he said, "Yep, it's all here."

You see, Philip wouldn't have even made it to the banana without a larger resource than what he possessed. And neither will you.

You are not whistling in the dark, hoping by some chance that your son might come back to the Lord, or your daughter's marriage be restored, or that your grandkids will find their way to the cross. You are being swept along by the tsunami of the provision of Heaven. He loves your family more than you do. He gave everything He had to make a place for them. So, give Him the wallet, and rely on the resources of your Heavenly Father.

Your Transferred Expectation

It is one of the great sagas of the Bible. I dare say one of the most used stories ever told. It has the sweep of longing, waste, jealousy, repentance, loneliness, in just a few verses.

Long before the boy left home, he had exercised in his mind, what he was going to do, what he was going to say and where he was going to go. He laid in his bed and had an imaginary discussion with his dad, trying to put the best face on a situation he knew would break his father's heart.

He finally sprung the trap and, before it was over, he had taken half of his father's wealth, turned from home carelessly and rode away to find himself and leave the shadow of his older brother far behind. Where he ended up, was a far different place than his vision that first day. The Bible tells us in Luke 15:11-31 that he wasted his substance. Another translation tells us, He spent all his money on prostitutes and parties.

I've watched many prodigals come and go. I've heard a thousand excuses and reasons. But the end destination is almost always the same place. At first, as the prodigal son failed and began his downward spiral, it didn't matter. He had plenty of money. Then it matters a little. As his "good times friends" disappeared with his father's fortune, somewhere along the line, he woke up and knew he had blown it.

All the while, back home, the father had a fatted calf. A fatted calf is only a fatted calf for a season, and then it becomes cattle. The fatted calf was a delicacy. Every morning, the old man got up, got dressed, stepped outside into the warmth of the day and asked a question, "Have you fed the calf?"

From the day his boy left, nothing to the father was the same. The fields were not important; neither were the cattle. The elder son took care of that. The father's only interest was the fatted calf. He'd leave his home and walk up to the end of the road where he last saw his beautiful son ride away with pride. Standing alone, on warm days and cold, in sun and rain, a father was looking for something.

You don't see someone far off by accident. To dim eyes, it requires concentration. I don't know how many fatted calves came and went, or how many days were spent looking down that road. But, one day, transferred expectation landed in a pig pen with a broken boy.

He wanted to fight the pigs for food. The pig is the epitome of filth and uncleanliness to the Jew. To be amongst them ruined his inheritance. I'm sure he was put amongst the pigs by his employer as a last and final cut into the soul of this young Jewish boy. He wanted to eat husks.

The Bible says there was a famine in the land, yet there were husks and pigs. The famine was in the boy. There is nothing more devoid of life; nothing is emptier than a prodigal son who is far from home. Your boy doesn't need for you to tell him how bad he is. Your daughter doesn't need a lecture. The greatest power they need to feel is the power of transferred expectation.

He sat there in tattered clothes, covered in the feces of pigs, fighting for a piece of rotten corn. Expectation met reality in a flash of revelation. HE CAME TO HIMSELF. Every time you pray, every time you confess, and every time you tell someone you believe God is saving your family, it sends a shockwave through the foundations of the prison that is holding your kids.

The father stood there looking down an empty road, on the edge of his nerves, at the extremity of his eyesight, screaming from his heart, "You've got to come home!" The power of transferred expectation crossed miles, melted shame, overcame hunger and loneliness, and the filth of a pigpen.

It first came as a whisper out of the prodigal's mouth, "I'm going home."

Take two photographs of this scene, two seconds apart. On the face of it, nothing is different, but the reality of it is that EVERYTHING has changed. There are still pigs; there are still rotten corn husks, there is still a tattered robe. But transferred expectation has transformed tragedy into reconciliation.

He straightens his shoulders, and talks to the pigs, "I am going home." He stands up. His feet are still in the filth of the pigpen. He announces to his audience, "I AM GOING HOME." And miles away, leaning on a post, peering down the road is a dad.

The boy had spent money, but his substance was still intact. He was a son. Reading this book, your son may be in a pigpen. Your family may have made its bed in Hell, but I dare you right now to lift your voice, and tell those that are absent, "You are coming home!"

From the north, "You are coming home!" From the south, "You are coming home!" From the east, "You are coming home!" From the west, "You are coming Home!

Release it now. The power of *transferred expectation*.

Your Transferred Forgiveness

It was just another day. He got up, got dressed, and asked the question, "Have you fed the calf?" He walked up to the end of the farm, leaned on the same post and looked. Across the rise of the road, he saw a distant figure. His heart raced faster. He had stood here for how long, we don't know. He had dreamed of the reunification of his family. He replayed, over and over in his mind, what he would say. But, he could never expect to see what he was about to see. He looked again, and this time the figure was clearer, and his heart sank. It isn't him.

He squints his eyes. He blinks, and the image is gone. He raises his hand, to give shadow from the sun, and peers more intently.

He looked down at the ground, disappointment washing over him. "It looks like a tramp coming to beg for food," he thought. His expectation lowered and he looked away. But something in his heart made him look again. "While he was yet a far way off, he saw him." Stooped and disheveled, with tattered robes and bare feet. The arrogance of youth had been beaten out of him by the bitterness of loneliness and hunger. But his dad recognized who he was through the mess he was in.

Elderly Jewish men do not run. But when your son shows up through the heat shimmer of a dusty road, the old father ran, and ran.

It doesn't tell us if the prodigal ran. He wasn't important. The story isn't about a rebellious kid; it's about the Father's love.

And he ran some more.

And when he got to the smelly, beaten son, still stinking of the pigs he had left behind, he didn't recoil in righteous anger and lecture his son on the money he had wasted, or the time that had been lost. He identified the young man as who he saw him to be. He kissed him and carried him home, and put on the failed son a ring, robes, and shoes which identified him as an heir of all things.

Another chorus that sings inside me as I write this, "When God He looks at me, He no more sees the things I've done. He only sees the Blood of His Crucified Son."

You see, God sent his Son amongst pigs that slaughtered him, without mercy or remorse. He stood for an eternity while His Son lay in a cold dark grave. He looked a far way off and saw through stone to the broken body of His only begotten. But when the time came, no demons, no devil, no science, no decay could stop that Son from rising from the grave.

The power of transferred forgiveness is working in you. God can forgive them for what they have done, but they will never find a safe place – they will never come to themselves if all there is a lecture and another beating from our self-righteous tongue. Give them a place to come. You don't have to tell them about pigs, hunger, nor loneliness. They need to know that the moment they decide to rise somebody, because of God's *transferred forgiveness,* is waiting for them.

Seed The Need

You do not need to be a farmer to know that to reap barley; you must sow barley. It would be silly to sow one thing and expect to reap another. An old verse says, *"There is a law that runs through life, you gather what you sow ~ You cannot plant a thistle, and expect a rose to grow."*

We have already said that what you feed your mind affects your spiritual effectiveness. This is also true of sowing and reaping. If you sow good seed in your inner man, you will reap a harvest of strength of character, motivation, and stability.

This portion of Scripture tells us to "be not weary in well-doing," and to "faint not." You may wait a long time for harvest time to come around. Things may be getting desperate in the situations you face, but keep sowing ~ the harvest is on its way! It might seem easier to give up and look for some shortcut which might conveniently happen along. But if it means compromise, if it means sowing bad seed, then leave the shortcuts to the others. "Faint not" is just another way of saying, "resist." If we determine in our hearts to live by the Word of God and to sow "to the Spirit," we will be equipping ourselves with exactly the right requirements to resist the enemy and to keep him out of our field. *He that soweth to the Spirit shall of the Spirit reap life everlasting.* That's life everlasting for you, and for everyone in your field!

Chapter Seven

The Promise Of Household Salvation

—ɯ—

I have shared with you the miraculous way in which God transformed the Cameron family. His sovereign power brought our whole family into a marvellous relationship with Him, but there is something which you must understand here. There was nothing special about the Camerons, except perhaps a huge appetite for sin. There was no logical reason on Earth why God should have moved in our family. He simply took us as we were, and loved us, and poured out His life-changing grace in our lives.

The Scripture says: *"...God is no respecter of persons"* (Acts 10:34). I believe with all my heart that what God did for our family, He is more than willing to do for yours. The first thing we must establish is that God's Word has put the issue beyond all doubt – Household Salvation has been promised to you! We must know this promise, and we must claim it and live our lives in expectancy of the day when everyone in our family will be rejoicing in this wonder of full salvation. IT'S TIME FOR HOUSEHOLD SALVATION.

Read this passage of Scripture carefully:

"Speak ye unto all the congregation of Israel, saying, In the tenth day of this month they shall take to them every man a lamb, according to the house of their fathers, a lamb for a house: And if the household be too little for the lamb, let him and his neighbour next unto his house take it ac-cording to the number of the souls: every man accord-ing to his eating shall make your count for the lamb. Your lamb shall be without blemish, a male of the first year: Ye shall take it out from the sheep, or from the goats: And ye shall keep it up until the fourteenth day of the same month: and the whole assembly of the congregation of Israel shall kill it in the evening. And they shall take of the blood, and strike it on the two side posts and on the upper door post of the houses, wherein they shall eat. And they shall eat the flesh in that night, roasted with fire and unleavened bread: and with bitter herbs they

shall eat it. Eat not of it raw, nor sodden at all with water, but roasted with fire; his head with his legs, and with the purtenance thereof. And ye shall let nothing of it remain until the morning; and that which remaineth of it until the morning ye shall burn with fire. And thus, shall ye eat it; with your loins girded, your shoes on your feet, and your staff in your hand; and ye shall eat it in haste: it is the LORD'S passover. For I will pass through the land of Egypt this night, and will smite all the first-born in the land of Egypt, both man and beast; and against all the gods of Egypt I will execute judgment: I am the Lord. And the blood shall be to you for a token upon the houses where ye are: and when I see the blood, I will pass over you, and the plague shall not be upon you to destroy you when I smite the land of Egypt." (Exodus 12:3-13).

Here we read of the origins of the Jewish feast of Passover. Moses had been raised up by God to deliver the children of Israel out of their bondage to the Egyptians. Time after time God had performed mighty signs and wonders through Moses to show Pharaoh that

God was moving on behalf of Israel. But Pharaoh refused to listen, for the Lord had hardened his heart, and he would not let the children of Israel go free. So, Moses delivered his warning from God that judgment was on its way. An angel of death would come. He would slay all the firstborn in every house. The only ones who would escape this awesome fate would be the children of Israel, but even they would only escape if they followed the Lord's instruction to the letter.

They were to take a lamb, kill it, and with a bunch of hyssop dipped in the lamb's blood; they were to strike the lintel and doorposts of their houses. This is the term which was used, and it thrills my heart every time I read it: *"A lamb for a house."*

Once the blood had been spread on the lintel and doorposts of that house, every single individual inside that home would be safe when the death angel passed over.

"When I see the blood," the Bible says, "I will pass over you, and the plague shall not be upon you to destroy you."

Can't you see it? If the blood of an ordinary lamb was enough to ensure safety for an entire household under the old dispensation, how much more will the blood of the Lamb of God, shed on Calvary, make provision for salvation for you and your house?

Back in Chapter Ten of Exodus, Moses said something wonderful. Pharaoh had tried to get Moses to leave Egypt with only the men. Finally, he tried to get the children of Israel to leave behind all their cattle. But Moses was determined that every man, woman, boy, girl, and even their livestock, would march triumphantly out of Egypt. *There shall not a hoof be left behind* "(Exodus 10:26).

Oh, that Christians today would be similarly determined that not one single member of our families will be left in the devil's kingdom. We can take them all to Glory with us if we begin to accept and claim God's promise of Household Salvation.

Rahab the Harlot
The Woman Who Saved Her Household

Rahab may have been known as a harlot, but she was, in fact, a woman who proved to be determined to bring the blessing of God upon her entire household. Her story in Joshua Chapter Two is one of the most moving examples of God's response to simple faith in Him.

Joshua was about to lead the children of Israel into the Promised Land. Standing as the prime obstacle to the fulfillment of all their dreams was the walled, fortress-like city of Jericho. The "City of Palms," they called it. As a strategic city where three of the main ancient trading routes converged, its capture was vital to the progress of the Israelites into the Promised Land.

Its 30-foot high double-walls stood in awesome defiance of any prospective attacker. This was going to be no easy task; the outer wall was six-feet thick, and the inner was 12-feet thick. A miracle was needed – and the Lord began to arrange circumstances to prepare for exactly that.

Joshua sent two spies into Jericho to assess the enemy's strength. Somehow the spies were spotted, and the King of Jericho sent his soldiers to capture them from the house where they had taken lodgings – the house of Rahab, the harlot.

Rahab, instead of turning the men over, as one might have expected her to do in response to a command from no less a person than the king himself, hid them on the roof of her house. Carefully, she covered the men with stalks of flax. Some of those stalks had been over a yard long, and up to an inch in diameter, so a few well-placed bundles would have afforded a perfect hiding place.

When the soldiers arrived, she told them that the men had been with her, but that they had since left. *"Pursue after them quickly, for ye shall over-take them,"* she said, misleading the king's soldiers.

You might be asking yourself why she took such a risk. The answer to that question is found in verse nine:

"And she said unto the men, I know that the Lord hath given you the land, and that your terror is fallen upon us, and that all the inhabitants of the land do faint because of you."

Rahab was simply aware that if God was moving on behalf of these people, then there was nothing anyone could do to stop them. She also realized a judgment day was coming. Rahab's later rescue can be attributed to the fact that she believed God, while the others in the city did not. Her faith was such that it merits her inclusion in God's "Hall of Faith" in Hebrews Chapter Eleven. She continues to show this faith to the two spies by saying *". . . for the Lord your God, He is God in Heaven above, and in the Earth beneath "*(Joshua 2:11).

Rahab boldly extracted a promise from the two spies, that in return for the kindness she had shown them, they would save alive her father's house when they returned with the armies of Israel to destroy Jericho: *"...save alive my father, and my mother, and my brethren, and my sisters, and all that they have, and deliver our lives from death"* (Joshua 2:13).

What a marvelous example of how we should feel about our families' salvation. Rahab was determined that every single person connected with her would be saved. Later in Chapter Six, when we read of the capture of Jericho, we find that Joshua indeed saved Rahab and *"her father's household, and all that she had"* (Joshua 6:25).

The little house must have been packed to the ceiling with Rahab's loved ones. It may be that many of them had not loved her, but we are not asked to pray only for those who love us, but for those who despitefully use us.

As a sign, whereby the Israeli army of would know Rahab's house, she was to tie the scarlet cord that she had used to let the spies down from her rooftop, from her window. That scarlet cord speaks to us of the blood of our Savior, still freely flowing, still availing for sin, and still able to secure salvation for you and your house.

Can you imagine the scene? Rahab is scurrying around trying to persuade her family to come to her house. She had been sworn to secrecy, so she could not tell them why. It is quite conceivable that there were some members of Rahab's family who weren't even on speaking terms with their "harlot" relative. But black sheep or not, Rahab threatened, begged and cajoled her family into coming to her house. Remember also, that she had no idea how long it would be until the Israelites would come. Her little house must have been packed tight with people from the moment the spies left.

A woman who had compromised every moral fiber of her being, changed both her priorities and her lifestyle to accommodate the many members of her family whom she wanted to be saved.

Rahab could have asked those two spies for anything. She was talking to people who could soon control the city and all its riches, but she had no thought for gold or fine garments. Her only concern was for the saving of her household.

Rahab was saved and lived the rest of her days with the children of Israel. The Scripture tells us that she married a man name Salmon (Matthew 1:5). Tradition has it that he was one of those same two spies who came to Jericho. Reading in Matthew Chapter One, we find that Salmon and Rahab are in the direct lineage of the One who would provide the means of salvation for *every* household.

Rahab a harlot and a Gentile through her determined faith in the God of Israel, not only saved her entire household, but became an Earthly ancestor of the Savior of the world, Jesus Christ.

With God on your side, anything can happen. Your background doesn't matter; neither does the enormity of the problem you face. What matters is the depth of your trust in the Lord God, who is God in Heaven above and in the Earth beneath.

Can God save your family? Of course, He can! Is He interested? Does He care about you and yours? Of course, He does! God who can take a harlot and place her in the royal lineage of the King of Kings, can take you and bless you with full Household Salvation ~ IT'S TIME!

Noah ~ The Man Who Prepared An Ark To Save His Household

Hebrews 11:7 reads: "By faith Noah, being warned of God of things not seen as yet, moved with fear, prepared an ark to the saving of his house..."

I'm sure that we are all familiar with the story of Noah and the ark, but it bears mentioning here because again we are brought face to face with God's desire that all of us should be concerned with our household. Not only that, but we are shown what it is that motivated Noah. In fact, it also motivated Moses and Rahab in their particu-lar situations.

Noah was moved with fear. His fear was born out of the knowledge that something was soon to occur for which he had to prepare his family. Moses knew it was coming, and so did Rahab. What was it? It was judgment! It is all very wonderful for preachers and teachers to minister about the goodness of God and all His many blessings, but we cannot afford to forget the other side of the coin. The Scripture says: "Behold therefore the goodness and severity of God..." (Romans 11:22).

We must never forget that God's judgment is real, and if we do not win our loved ones to Christ, then they will have to face that judgment. The final judgment for sin is Hell, and at that point, all the joking stops. I have already shared with you how God left me in no doubt as to the savage reality of the fate of those who die in their sins. We do not have time to waste! We must reach our loved ones for Christ – NOW! IT IS TIME.

One of the most graphic statements I have ever read is found in Genesis 7:16; "And the Lord shut him in." It wasn't Noah who shut the door of the ark; it was God who shut the door. Noah had stood for righteousness amid a perverse generation. All the time that Noah had been building the ark, the people had the opportunity to repent and turn to God. But when the moment came, when God finally decided that it was time for judgment, He closed the door to His mercy and all mankind, except those in the ark, were destroyed.

We must face the fact that God's judgment is again going to come upon this earth. That's why my watchword has become, "IT'S TIME." It isn't just a slogan, a nice logo for people to recognize our ministry by. It is a truth of which I become more aware with every passing day. IT'S TIME – FOR HOUSEHOLD SALVATION.

Household Salvation in the Book of Acts

The theme of "Household Salvation" runs right through the New Testament. One of the places where it comes through strongly is the Book of Acts, in which we read of God laying the foundations of His Church.

In Acts, we see numerous thrilling instances of God showing us that salvation is not only for us, but also for our households.

In Acts 11:13-14 we read, *". . . call for Simon, whose surname is Peter; who shall tell thee words, whereby thou and all thy house shall be saved."* In a strange sort of way, I feel a bit like that. God has shown me to tell people everywhere, words whereby they and all their houses can be saved.

I want to make sure that you understand that the words which you are reading on these pages are more than just good ideas—they are God ideas. God wants you to be saved, *and your house.*

Further, in Acts 16:14, we are introduced to Lydia, a woman whose heart the Lord opened, who attended unto the things which were spoken of Paul. The following verse tells us that this results in her being baptized, along with her household. In the same chapter,

Paul and Silas are gloriously visited by the power of God while in prison. Their bands were loosed. The jailer, rushed in, and began to commit suicide, thinking that the prisoners had escaped. Paul cried out to him, *"Do thyself no harm: for we are all here."*

Falling before Paul and Silas, he asked that most marvelous question: *"Sirs, what must I do to be saved?"*

Paul's answer has thrilled the souls of men and women since it was spoken: *"Believe on the Lord Jesus Christ, and thou shalt be saved, and thy house"* (Acts 16:31).

The story continues: *"And they spoke unto him the Word of the Lord, and to all that were in his house. And he took them the same hour of the night, and washed their stripes; and was baptized,* he and all his, *straightway"* (verses 32-33).

What a wonderful salvation this is! God's heart of love is not content to stop with you alone changed and blessed by His power. He won't rest until He gets you to realize that you can see your whole family share in the marvel of redemption. IT'S TIME for "Household Salvation."

It's Your Right

This must be made completely clear; I am not just telling you that it is possible for your family to be saved. I am telling you that *it is your God-given right* to expect salvation for your whole household. I have shown you how God did it in my family, and what God's Word says about it. There is no room for argument. Household Salvation has been promised to you. *It is your right.*

The reason that many of our loved ones are still unsaved is that we have not claimed God's promise; we have not directed our faith toward God on behalf of our families.

I should point out here that I am not suggesting that you embark on a campaign of nagging and badgering your relatives to receive Christ. That would neither help you, nor them. But by living a godly life before them, even if they abuse you, and by fully expecting by faith that God will move to bring them in, things will begin to happen. God will turn the situation around.

When life begins to deal its hard blows to them, be ready for them to come to you for the help they need.

God will show you opportunities beyond your imagination to prove to them His power will work in your life. It works! ITS TIME for you to see it work for you! Again—Household Salvation is your right!

We have seen from the Scriptures how God has made Household Salvation part of the package for every Christian. As you read on, I intend to show you some of the specific things that you can do to see it become a reality in your life. I pray that you have already begun to realize that God is, even now, moving on your behalf.

You have already begun the process whereby God will bring them in. If you are willing to trust God and believe His Word, you can be truly sure that IT'S TIME—for Household Salvation.

Chapter Eight
Here's What You Can Do

—ᛘ—

From what we have discovered so far, we can see a plan emerging which, if we follow, will cause us to take giant steps forward in bringing our entire families to Christ.

Let's look further at the processes involved in achieving Household Salvation.

1. Resist The Devil And Drive Him From The Field Of Your Life.

We have gone into this in some detail, but we should realize that there is much more to defeating Satan than just reading a few pages in a book. You can put a book on the shelf and forget about it. However, you cannot afford to leave valuable knowledge on a shelf; you must use it effectively. All the learning in the world will do us no good if we fail to incorporate it into our everyday lives. Therefore, it is not enough for us to agree that we should resist the devil; we must ensure that next time we deal with him, we *do resist him*.

Most people will nod their head in agreement with the steps to resisting Satan which we have discussed. They will say "amen" to such propositions as knowing it is God who is in control or giving total effort to the fight or continuing instant in prayer. But we must do more than agree; we must ACT! If we are serious about bringing our families to the Lord, we are going to have to be certain that we form the daily habitual process of driving Satan from our fields.

I cannot emphasize this enough. To resist Satan requires more than good intentions, or to mentally accept some "magic formula." It needs action ~ conscious, deliberate action. Neither the intention nor the desire to resist Satan will budge him one inch. But, when you take authority over him by the power of the Holy Spirit in you, and resist him in the name of Jesus, he will FLEE.

1.   Be Aware of Impending Judgment

If we forget the reality of Hell, and that its torment awaits those of our loved ones who die in their sins, we will lose our motivation to win them to the Lord. Rahab knew that judgment was coming to Jericho and it prompted her to move into action to save her household.

Noah was "moved with fear," and he built an ark to save his house.

We must never forget two things. One is that Hell is real, and the other is that the end of this age is imminent. We need to burn those facts into our minds every day. Just as we cannot forget to resist the devil, neither can we forget the horror and irrevocability of a sentence to eternal damnation.

Again, however, we need more than mere words. It is action we need. Ask yourself every day, "Am I doing all I can with this day's opportunities to ensure that my loved ones don't end up in Hell?"

2. Claim The Unclaimed Promise

When we begin to resist the devil, we will soon discover the value of prayer. If we intend to see our families come to Christ, we must begin to immediately pull down the strongholds of Satan through an active and determined prayer life.

As we pray concerning our households, our faith will be greatly encouraged if we will rejoice in God's promises. We need to absorb these promises into our spirit and begin to claim them for ourselves. God's promises are to you! Live as though you believe them!

One key factor here is an overcoming perseverance which refuses to stop praying and refuses to stop believing, despite situations which may even appear to be growing worse.

My mother prayed for seven years, which is a long time to pray. My father's determination to break her grew stronger by the day, but he didn't break mother, God broke him.

My aunt Chrissie, who was saved on that same marvelous evening with my mother, was married to a man named Charlie. She prayed for him for over twenty years. Like my Dad, Charlie would fly off the handle every time Chrissie mentioned Jesus. One day, after he had been quite ill for some time, Chrissie looked at him as he sat in his chair. He appeared somehow to be distressed. She thought, "I would love to ask him just one more time if he would like to be saved, but I know it will just cause a scene."

Then Chrissie heard the voice of the Lord speak softly to her: "Go ahead, ask him one more time." So, Chrissie knelt by the side of Charlie's chair and did as the Lord told her.

"Charlie," she said, "don't you think it's time you got saved?"

Tears immediately began to stream down Charlie's face. "Oh Chrissie," he sobbed, "I thought you would never ask."

Charlie, who had been so hard and hostile, wept his way to Calvary and was transformed by God's love.

Chrissie could have given up; she could have said, "No, I don't want to risk another argument," but she knew the voice of God and she knew the promise of God. God moved in Chrissie's impossible situation, and He certainly can move in yours.

Remember, don't stop believing. Don't give up praying and claiming your promise. It's always too soon to quit!

While we need to persevere, and win our families – whatever it takes – God is about to do a quick work.

Through our television and radio ministry, people have been calling and writing in prayer requests for their unsaved loved ones from all over the U.S.A. and Canada. Some of them have been praying for their family members for years, yet it seems so many have discovered that their very act of faith, in writing or calling, has been the catalyst for miracles in their lives.

Amazingly, some people were calling back to us within hours of their first call for prayer, to say that God had supernaturally saved their loved ones.

It can happen for you, so begin to believe. Claim that promise now. IT'S TIME!

3. Let God Do It His Way

We humans have an incredible tendency to interfere with things that are none of our business. I am certainly not saying that the salvation of our households is none of our business, but how God brings it to pass depends on His wisdom, not ours.

When my son Philip was a young boy, he went through a stage which I suppose all little boys go through. He wanted to do everything by himself to prove his independence and ability. Even in the simple matter of combing his hair, he was determined to make sure he lent a hand. I would try to comb his hair, and his hands would be everywhere trying to help. Eventually, I had to pin his arms to his sides by holding him between my knees, and then quickly do the job.

Invariably, he would wriggle one hand free, and just as I finished, he would say, "Me do it, Daddy." A little hand would shoot up like lightning, finding its way to his hair, where he would begin to "comb" with his fingers.

Somehow, I think God must face the same problem with us. Just as He is getting ready to do what we have prayed so hard for, we decide to lend a hand. Like the famous bull in a china shop, we barge into things that would work out so much better if we would just leave it to the Lord. We don't help matters one bit by nagging. For instance, if an unsaved husband is drinking, perhaps a wife might find herself plunging into despair because, "Oh, dear, he's drinking again."

Certainly, it isn't good news that he's drinking again, but it isn't going to help anything if we get depressed and lose our faith-grip on God's promises, or if we "pitch a holy fit" and start lecturing him about what a bad boy he's been. He is acting that way because he is unsaved. He does not understand the need to conform to the standards of a spiritual life. If you nag and fuss, you may create a bigger problem because of the barrier of resentment which can be built up. It is, of course, necessary to be there, to love, to advise and, through the life you lead, to show the way to a better answer than can be found from a bottle or anything else. Just to set the record straight, let me say that men can be pretty good too when it comes to nagging. If you don't believe me, ask my wife! I'm joking (a little), but please don't miss the point.

If we will concentrate on our walk with God, and present a Christianity which is real, and not some ethereal, mystical, far-away-look-in-the-eyes religion, we can get through to our loved ones in a much more effective fashion.

God knows exactly the circumstances we are in. None of our difficulties take Him by surprise. When He wants to move upon the hearts of your loved ones, He will enter right into their situation. He will speak to them clearly in their terms, in a way which will leave them in no doubt about His love and power.

When the Lord told Peter to launch out into the deep and to let down his nets, all Peter's instincts told him it was folly. (Luke 5:3, 11) He had been working all night. He was a fisherman. He knew every good fishing spot in the region. Yet, his experience had been to no effect. How could this stranger, this carpenter's son, know more than he? Didn't he know that you don't catch fish in the daytime? Nevertheless, he obeyed – and Peter and his men collected so many fish that they filled two boats to the point that they were in danger of sinking.

Nothing could have spoken to Peter more clearly than this. He knew that only Divine forces could have produced this miracle, and brought so many fish to where there had been none the whole night long.

The miracle's immediate effect on Peter was to convict him of his sin. *"Depart from me; for I am a sinful man, O Lord,"* he said. (Luke 5:8) From that point, Peter became a disciple of the Lord Jesus, and he was never the same again. I believe with all my heart that God is just as able to get right down to where your loved ones are living and talk to them in their language. God will show them just as clearly that He can move mightily in their circumstances.

What we must do is to watch for the "special, anointed moment," and be ready to act, just as Aunt Chrissie was when the Lord told her to ask one more time."

Allow God to do the job His way! You can't alter the situation by worrying, by fretting or by fussing. We can alter it by praying, by believing and by trusting God to keep His promise of Household Salvation.

4. Let God's Nature Motivate You.

We must understand that God's heart of love is such that it is His desire to save every single member of our families.

He will bless you because of your concern for your household. When Lot was rescued out of Sodom, it wasn't because of anything that Lot himself had done. It was because of faithful Abraham's forceful intercession. Lot was rescued, but Abraham's blessings were innumerable. He learned how to commune with God and walk in the knowledge of the power of prayer. He became "father of the faithful."

God is displeased when we fail to take our Scriptural responsibilities in respect of our family. The Word of God says: *But if any provide not for his own, and especially for those of his own house, he hath de-nied the faith, and is worse than an infidel"* (1 Timothy 5:8). These are strong words indeed.

Your Concern Is Only
A Fraction Of My Concern

My father tells of an incident that happened to him as he was traveling one day by car near Los Angeles. His brother, Alex, was driving, so Dad took the opportunity to have a time of inward meditation and prayer. As he did, he began to think of some of our relatives back in Scotland who had still not come to Christ.

He began to pray, "Lord, I'm so worried about my family. It hurts me to hear of them still bound by sin." Some of them were, in fact, often to be seen staggering down the street in a drunken and near-paralytic state. "Lord," he continued, "I'm so concerned about my household."

Dad began to feel the Spirit of the Lord move upon his heart and say to him, "Son, you have said that you are concerned about YOUR house-hold, but I want you to know that your concern is only a fraction of my concern. If you are concerned about YOUR household, know that I am concerned about MY household, and I am working now to move upon their hearts."

Whenever God touches your heart about the spiritual needs of your family, you also touch His. His very nature is to love, save and transform.

We see the nature of God in Jesus' reaction to the cries of Mary and Martha as they mourned the loss of Lazarus. At the same time, they expressed great faith: *"Lord, if thou hadst been here, my brother would not have died."* (John 11:32).

How did Jesus react? He wept. He was so involved in this family situation, so touched by the love of Mary and Martha for their brother that He wept. He not only wept, but He also raised Lazarus from the dead.

If you have not realized it – Jesus cares for you and your family. He cares enough to promise that if you remain faithful to Him, He will save your entire household.

The nature of God is such that you can move Him because your concern evokes His concern, your love evokes His love – and His love will change your family!

Taking this thought a step further, we should take time now and then to marvel at the wonder of the character and nature of our Lord. In Isaiah, we read:

"Behold, my servant shall deal prudently; he shall be exalted and extolled, and be very high.

"As many as were astonied at thee ~ His visage was so marred more than any man, and His form more than the sons of men."

"So, shall He sprinkle many nations; the kings shall shut their mouths at Him: for that which had not been told them shall they see; and that which they had not heard, shall they consider."

The word used in verse 14 is *"astonied,"* an old-English word meaning astonished. The prophet is trying to tell us something. The nature of Christ is so marvelous, so indescribably wonderful, that it is simply *astonishing!* If we want our loved ones to fall in love with Jesus, we can never afford to lose our sense of astonishment at the lovely Nazarene.

He is so astonishing! We read here, that kings shut their mouths at Him. He is so astonishing, that when He came to town, He put the doctors out of business. The Bible says, *"He healed them all"* (Matthew 12:15).

He is so astonishing that He could die on the cross, and turn death and seeming defeat into the very means of life and victory for all mankind.

He is so astonishing that He could promise, *"Believe on the Lord Jesus Christ, and thou shalt be saved, –* and thy house."* (Acts 16:31).

So be astonished. Be enraptured by the person of Christ. Be willing to let Him turn your concern for your family into the blessing of a closer walk with Him for you, and the miracle of Household Salvation upon all your entire household. Let the nature of God motivate you!

Below, I have simply listed some key Scriptures to help you believe for Household Salvation. I know that you will come across many more in your studies. However, these will form a good starting point:

Deuteronomy 7:9: *"Know therefore that the Lord thy God, He is God, the faithful God, which keepeth covenant and mercy with them that love Him and keep His commandments to a thousand generations."*

Hebrews 6:17: *"God also bound Himself with an oath, so that those He promised to help would be* perfectly sure and never need to wonder whether He might change His plans (Living Bible)."

Proverbs 13:22: "A good man leaveth an inheri-tance to his children's children: and the wealth of the sinner is laid up for the just."

Isaiah 54:13: "And all thy children shall be taught of the Lord; and great shall be the peace of your children."

II Corinthians 1:20: "For all the promises of God in Him are yea, and in Him Amen, unto the glory of God by us."

Psalm 103:17,18: "But the lovingkindness of the Lord is from everlasting to everlasting, to those who reverence Him; His salvation is to children's children of those who are faithful to His covenant and remember to obey Him (Living Bible)."

Jeremiah 2:9: "But I will not give you up ~ I will plead for you to return to me, and will keep on pleading; even with your children's children in the years to come! (Living Bible)."

I Samuel 2:35: "Then will I raise up a faithful priest who will serve me and do whatever I tell him to do. I will bless his descendants, and his family shall be priests to my kings forever. (Living Bible)."

Acts 10:2: "A devout man, and one that feared God WITH ALL HIS HOUSE, which gave much alms to the people, and prayed to God always."

Acts 16:31: "...Believe on the Lord Jesus Christ, and thou shalt be saved, and thy house."

Luke 19:9: "And Jesus said unto him, This day is salvation come to this house, forsomuch as he also is a son of Abraham."

Luke 8:39: "Return to thine own house, and show how great things God hath done unto thee: And he went his way, and published throughout the whole city, how great things Jesus had done unto him."

Exodus 12:3: "Speak ye unto all the congrega-tion of Israel, saying, In the tenth day of this month they shall take to them every man a lamb, according to the house of their fathers, a lamb for a house."

Acts 11:13,14: "...Call for Simon, whose sur-name is Peter; Who shall tell thee words, whereby thou and all they house shall be saved."

Acts 16:14,15: *"And a certain woman named Lydia, a seller of purple, of the city of Thyatira, which worshiped God, heard us: whose heart the Lord opened, that she attended unto the things which were spoken of Paul. And when she was baptized, and her household, she besought us saying, If ye have judged me to be faithful to the Lord, come into my house and abide there. And she constrained us."*

This chapter does not deal with *everything* you can do about achieving Household Salvation, but if you put these principles into practice in your life, I am convinced that you will set in motion the forces of Heaven to work on your behalf. And remember – IT'S TIME!

Chapter Nine

Mothers: God's Secret Weapon

—◦◦◦—

One of God's secret weapons in His plan to bring Household Salvation to the Church is the praying, Bible-believing mother, who refuses to let the devil have her children.

From experience, I can say that I could not begin to think where I would be today if my mother had not been the kind of woman who wanted, above all else, to see her family living for God.

They say that the most valuable evidence in a courtroom is that provided by an eyewitness. I am not writing this because it seems to be a good theory, or because I have heard someone else share a message which seems to fit my ministry. I write this as a personal testimony to the awesome difference that a godly mother makes.

As a young boy, I often considered what I wanted to be when I grew up. Sometimes it was a pilot, or railroad engineer, or a fireman, depending on what took my fancy at the time.

"That's good," my mother would say when I told her. "But let me tell you about someone."

She would then proceed to tell me stories of great men of God down through history. Each time I would reply by saying something like, "That's right, Mum, when I grow up, I'm going to a preacher like my Dad." Mum made sure that all my heroes were preachers, and none greater than my Dad.

I recall one time when I had traded some bubble gum cards for a poster of Jimi Hendrix, one of the big rock stars of the day. In my childish excitement, I took the poster home and ran up to my room. Carefully, I pinned my new treasure onto the old chipboard wall of my bedroom.

"Mum, come and look at this!" I shouted down the stairs to her. When she came into the room, I began to enthuse about the talents of my new idol. For a moment, there was silence. Then she spoke softly (how I would come to dread it when she spoke to me in that soft voice), "I wonder how many young people he'll be responsible for sending to Hell? If you want to leave the poster there, you can ~ the choice is yours. Your Dad is away preaching right now, winning people to Jesus. I don't think the man in the picture will ever do that. Do you?" With that, she left.

I stood there more stunned than if she had yelled at me and given me a sound thrashing. Looking at the poster on the wall, I began to get angry at myself for getting so wrapped up in someone whose only achievement in life was playing guitar. I tore the poster from the wall and ran downstairs. "Throw it in the garbage can, Mum," I said. "I don't want anything to do with it."

The Most Exciting Place In Town

Mum turned our house into a place everyone wanted to be. When I would meet my friends, and suggest that we go somewhere, they would invariably say, "No, let's go to your house instead." She turned our backyard into the most exciting place in town.

If we played football, she played football. If we did anything at all, she was right in the thick of it with us. She couldn't swim, but she took us to the pool and taught every one of us to swim. She taught me to box and to ride a bike.

Once, my cousin John and I decided to dig a hole from our backyard, according to our calculations, to Australia. Being Scottish, we would then, of course, charge a suitable fee to those who wanted to use our hole to take this amazing shortcut to the other side of the world. However, it wasn't very long before tired muscles got the better of us and we abandoned the project.

While we were resting from our labors, we decided to lay a trap for anyone who might have wanted to sabotage our hole. So, we perched a bucket of water above the door which led into the backyard.

You can imagine the sickening feeling which gripped my stomach when who should come through the door, but my mother. Down came the water and the bucket on top of her, just missing her head and drenching her to the skin.

For a moment, she looked surprised and bewildered; then her eyes seemed to say, "Wait till I find out who did that." Then, seeing our horror-stricken faces, she began to fall into uncontrollable laughter. Somewhat relieved, we began to laugh too until we were rolling on the ground in danger of falling into our newly dug hole.

On another occasion, my cousins, my sister and I built a little camp in the backyard. There was an old pear tree which grew out at the oddest of angles from the back wall of the yard. By carefully draping an old tarpaulin across its branches, we made a small shelter and packed it with everything we could fit into it. We had chairs, mattresses, and what we thought were all the comforts of home. Our plan was to spend the night there, but when it began to rain, we decided to "camp" on the floor of one of the rooms of the house instead. On the way out I knocked one of the candles, which we were using for light, onto one of the straw mattresses on the floor. I picked up the candle, blew it out and folded over the mattress, thinking I had taken care of the problem.

After we had settled down on the floor of our indoor campsite, my mother came in. "Did you kids put out the candles under the tarpaulin?" she asked.

"Yes Mum," I replied with confidence.

"Well, come look at this."

We followed her into the backyard where we saw our carefully constructed camp had become a roaring inferno, billowing forth columns of thick, black smoke.

What followed was another of those hilarious slapstick situations that had to be seen to be believed.

We tried to form a chain to carry buckets of water to put out the fire. One of my aunts preferred to run around with a little jug, spilling most of the water as she ran. Mayhem is not the word for it. It is honestly a miracle that we didn't burn the whole street down.

Faith Adventures

I came home one day from school. Down the four stairs into the kitchen and met my mom smiling, standing at the empty kitchen table. My sister Wendy had beaten me home and was standing beside her. My younger siblings, Neil and Louise were only glints in her eye. My mother laughed out loud when she saw me and then in a sentence destroyed the hope in her little boy's heart. "Philip, we have no money for supper." "And if we had, we have no money for gas." In those days, and maybe even still today, the poor folk would have a meter put in their homes, so that they could pay for the gas and electricity as they used it. Every three months the "gas" man or the "electricity" man would pay us a visit. He opened the meter and took out the shillings that we put in the slot over the last three months and counted. I can still see him sliding the coins across the top of the table into his hand. Twenty shillings to the pound. I just been told we neither had food nor a shilling for the meter. My amazing mom turned what was threatening to be a disaster into both a game and a challenge of faith. Back then, you bought tea loose into a quarter pound packet and attached to the label was a stamp. You would remove the stamp and put it in a cardboard stamp book and once you filled the book with stamps, you could get a shilling for all the stamps. It was a means by which you would be faithful to a certain brand of tea. Mom held the cardboard booklet in her hand and said if we can find three more stamps, we can fill this book up and get a shilling for the gas meter. The three of us, mom, Wendy and I ransacked our kitchen, every drawer, every box, every nook and cranny and I found the last one on a shelf. We had our shilling!!! She then looked at me and Wendy and said let's pray that God sends us a lodger so mom, me and Wendy knelt around a small stool in our kitchen. All our elbows on the small square wicker rattan stool. She looked at me and said, "Philip you pray." A little boy prayed this prayer. "Dear Jesus, our dad is somewhere preaching the Gospel. Please send someone to stay with us tonight so we can have supper." There was a knock on the door. My mom clapped her hands jumped up from her knees bounded up the four steps and with me and Wendy following close behind, she opened the glass door of our home to find the somewhat bewildered man gazing at this redhead with her two kids by her side. "Eh, do you take in lodgers?" "Yes," mom replied. "Do you have any rooms available?" "Yes," mom replied. He asked how much it was and said he would be there for 3 days. He then asked a question that made my heart stop. "Do you want me to pay you now or when I leave?" Mom replied, nonchalantly "Whenever you want." I held my breath. A shilling's worth of gas would not feed us. He reached into his pocket and took out the pound notes for three nights of lodging. Mom thanked him and took the money. She dropped the hand down by her side. I took the money from her hand, ran back down the four stairs into the back yard up the alley between our house and next door. I ran as fast as I could. Cardboard booklet in one hand and the money in the other. I got to the store ran by two brothers known as the Boggie brothers. My mother had a standing order with them. A list of groceries we would get. I breathlessly told them that I was there to get my mom's groceries. In a few minutes, I was running home. I ran back down the alley to the kitchen window, mom saw me, opened the window and I handed her the groceries and then I casually walked back inside the house. Supper, a miraculous supper, cooked by miraculous gas from the tea stamps we had found. We sat down and ate with our new lodger. He was putting in the floor in the new Woolworth's store. It was his first visit to our little town to inspect the job. He was coming back and would spend many months in our house. But that first night as mom poured tea from our sanctified "tea pot" and told the man how he had met our need. I was proud of my dad preaching the Gospel. I was proud of my mom for making a challenge into a game. I was proud of myself. I had found the last tea stamp to fill out the booklet. Your legacy of faith will indelibly mark your loved ones. As they see faith in you making a path for them.

The Rabbit Lesson

One day my Dad brought home a pet rabbit from one of his preaching trips. I could not have wished for anything better. Rabbits were the latest craze to hit our school and everyone, it seemed, had their own rabbit.

Well, now I had a rabbit, but nowhere to keep it. "Mum," I asked, "can we buy a rabbit's hutch?"

"Son," she replied, "You know that we don't have much money. We can't afford that right now." I begged, pleaded, yelled and tried everything to get her to say yes, but to no avail.

Finally, in a childish tantrum, I cried, "It isn't fair that I can't have it just because Dad wants to go away and preach. Everyone else can afford their own rabbit's hutch." With that, I slammed the door and went off to bed to sulk.

Next morning, I got up and went down to the kitchen, hardly remembering my temper the night before. I wasn't ready for the sight that awaited me when I opened the kitchen door. Mum had fallen asleep, crouching over something on the floor. She was holding an ax. She had been using the blunt end as a hammer. Underneath her was a newly finished rabbit's hutch, which she had just spent the whole night making out of small fruit boxes.

She woke with a start. By now I was in tears as I realized the trouble she had gone to, just to make sure that her boy wouldn't be able to say that he had to do without something because his Dad was a preacher.

"This is for you Philip," she said. I couldn't say anything as I realized how selfish I had been, and yet another spiritual lesson was etched in my heart.

A New Guitar

As I grew older, I wanted to learn to play a musical instrument. So, Mum bought me an old, cheap guitar. Today, I can play several instruments without much difficulty, but it was a different story then. In fact, there were those who assured her that I had no ear for music, and should forget trying to play anything.

However, I had inherited a good-sized streak of determination, and I persisted with my dream. "The day you can play a hymn on that guitar which I can recognize," my Mum promised, "I'll buy you a good guitar." That was all I needed.

I did have one problem, though. The neck of the guitar Mum had given me was just too big for my fingers to get around to playing it properly, so I had to come up with something fast. Where I got the inspiration for the idea I came up with next, I do not know. I somehow managed to lift out the magnifying glass from the gauge of a set of bath-room scales. By placing the guitar on my knees, and using the glass, I could play the guitar "Hawaiian" style. Eventually, I mastered a tune, and I proudly called in my Mum and Dad and played for them *The Old Rugged Cross.* Mum knew that a promise is a promise, and she assured me that I would get my guitar.

I will never forget the day they took me to a music shop in Aberdeen to buy my new guitar. They made me wait in our old van while they went into the shop. What I didn't know then was that the guitar cost thirty-two pounds and they had only sixteen. So, they had gone in first to avoid embarrassment in front of me because they did not know if the shop would approve them for credit. I remember crying with excitement as they brought the guitar out to me. The guitar cost my parents what, at the time, was a small fortune. The sacrifice, when I think of it now, was immense, but my Mum and Dad would never begrudge anything that we could use for the Lord's work. They spent no money on worldly entertainment, only on things for God.

A Mother's Wisdom

Over the years, I've discovered something about my Mum. She is the closest thing to omniscient that you will ever meet. Often, as a child, I would do something wrong, and before I even got home, she knew about it. She would just speak to me in that soft voice. I would cry out to her, "Smack me. Yell at me, but please don't talk to me in your soft voice."

Nowadays, I'm more grateful for her wisdom. I'm glad that, without saying a word, she knows what I'm thinking and when I'm hurting. If I need straightening out, though I'm no longer a little boy, Mum knows how to do it.

There is a saying, "The hand that rocks the cradle, rules the world." Mothers, the role you play in shaping your children for God could not be more vital.

I am only one of four children, all of whom are full-time in the Lord's work, and we can each tell our stories of how Mum molded us and directed our desires toward God.

So often, in modern society, the role of the mother is treated with disdain. Women are made to feel inadequate unless they go out and "do their own thing."

I cannot help but think that no one could achieve anything more satisfying, or worthy of greater honor than to bring up their children to know the power of God moving in their lives.

My mother used to pray, "Lord, I do not ask you for beauty, or for wealth, or for nice clothes, or any of those things. All I ask is that you allow me to bring my children up to serve you." She would ask God to so mark us with Himself that we would radiate Christ without being asked. "What's the point," she would say, "of going through the pain of giving birth (and she knew that only too well), of struggling to bring up your kids, only to hand them over to the devil when they grow up?"

You only need to own one small precious jewel to guard it carefully. How much more a child's life?

I often heard my mother praying by my bedside that God would cause me to grow up to serve Him. I would turn my head away. She wouldn't know I was awake and I would hear her weep for me before the Lord. I used to lie there with tears flowing down my cheeks, knowing that I could never be anything but what she prayed for me to be.

If you ever meet Wendy Cameron, you will instantly know that I haven't even begun to tell her story. God often uses Mum in the gift of healing. She knows what it is to minister under the anointing of God before thousands of people. When you talk to her, you will find that it won't be long before she begins to talk about her kids, and how the most important job of her life has been to create in them a hunger for God.

Mothers are God's secret weapon. Mother, you can alter the course of history by the way you yield to God when bringing up your children. The world needs more men and women of God. Whether the Lord gets them early in life might well depend on mothers who know how to listen to God, and *"train up a child in the way that he should go..."* For then, the Bible says, *"...when he is old, he will not depart from it."* (Proverbs 22:6). My mother set her heart and mind on Christ and geared everything in that direction. She constantly prayed that God would lead her.

Saved By A Mother's Love

Time after time in the Scriptures, we see God emphasize the vital role of mothers. My mind turns to the story of Moses, starting in Exodus chapter one. The decree had gone out:

"...Every son that is born ye shall cast into the river..." (Exodus 1:22). Surrounded by the screams of mothers as they saw their children drown before their eyes, a mother and daughter desperately planned a way of saving their son and brother. Other mothers had just given up and accepted the seemingly inevitable. This mother had decided to attempt to thwart Pharaoh's plan.

Meticulously, they prepared the tiny ark, filling every gap between the reeds with pitch. They diligently labored, even as death's hand fell all around them. God was on their side, and during the construction of the little craft, not one soldier approached their dwelling. You see, they were working according to the will of God.

How they managed to carry their precious burden to the river, we will never know, but I have found that faith creates its own opportunities.

At the water, they placed baby Moses in the ark. His mother went back to labor as a slave, manufacturing bricks for Pharaoh, as his sister stood silent vigil over her brother, against what seemed impossible odds.

Miriam could have panicked when she saw the Pharoah's daughter, the princess and her entourage, approach them. She could have done the wrong thing and caused death to come upon her entire family. Instead, she hid until the opportune moment. Swallowing her fear, the little slave girl approached the princess. With courage that only love can produce, and by deft negotiating, she not only saved her brother, but created a paying job for her mother to raise Moses.

I repeat, one of the greatest weapons in all the world is a mother's love. Hell cannot stop a praying, believing mother from achieving her aim when she decides to claim the promise of Household Salvation.

They never knew what Moses' call would be. They just loved this baby and refused to see him die. Today we know that Moses saw more miracles, apart from Jesus than anyone. But when he was helpless, his mother stood in the gap, and his sister refused to let her brother be lost.

Mothers, as Hell claims its estimated 6,000 souls per hour, stand and proclaim that none of your seed ~ no loved one of yours ~ will be lost. With a determination from God, withstand the power of Hell. By the power of the Blood of the Lamb, and the word of your testimony, see God move and bring them in.

Hannah Prays For A Son

The Bible shows that if you dedicate your children to God, the future can be filled with wonder. Those children can grow to know the blessing and power of God moving in their lives in ways that can surpass your highest dreams.

Elkanah's wife was Hannah. His other wife, Peninnah, had children, but Hannah was barren. We find the heart-broken woman grieving in the temple, crushed by the cruelty of Peninnah's taunting insults. So deeply wounded was she that she couldn't bring herself to speak aloud to God.

Eli, the old priest, saw her moving her lips, without making a sound, and thought, "she's drunk."

Hannah was not drunk. Rather, she had been swept away into intimate communion with God, and she made a vow: *"O Lord of hosts, if thou wilt indeed look on the affliction of thine handmaid... but wilt give unto thine handmaid, a man-child, then I will give him unto the Lord all the days of his life..."*(1 Samuel 1:11).

She declared that no razor would ever come near his head, signifying that her son would be of the order of the Nazarites. Like Samson before him, Hannah's child would be set apart, kept from strong drink and uncleanness, and wholly given over as one of God's special vessels. God answered the cry of Hannah's heart and gave her a son.

We can tell this story so glibly, and not fully appreciate the courage of character shown by Hannah. It wasn't easy to give her boy, Samuel, to Eli the priest, knowing that once done; she would have no more say in her son's future.

Nevertheless, she kept her bargain with God and handed Samuel over, not sure of what would become of him. We know that her faithfulness resulted in the emergence of a mighty prophet who would guide the children of Israel as the oracle of God.

That baby in your arms today, that tiny, helpless bundle, has a potential in God. Guide, mold, pray, teach and show, and God's boundless resources and power will flow to and through that child.

The choice is yours! *"Choose life that thou and thy seed may live"* (Deuteronomy 30:19).

Chapter Ten

Fathers

—m—

If the role of the mother is vital, it is even more crucial that the father knows how to play his part in bringing his family to experience full Household Salvation. Some fathers refuse to fulfill their spiritual obligation to their families and tie the mother's hands. Often, for apparently good and honorable, but nonetheless mistaken reasons, fathers can do irreparable damage to their children's zeal for God.

More money, a better job, a bigger home, comfort and plentiful provision for the family might sound like the best motivational forces for a father, but that can be wrong, and sometimes a fatal misconception. My father would never allow money or possessions to come between God and his children.

The book of Ruth tells of a man named Elimelech, whose name means, "God is King." His wife was Naomi, meaning "pleasantness."

This family man had two sons named Mahlon and Chilion. Scholarly opinion differs as to the meaning of their names, but I feel that the meanings, "a song" and "a sense of completeness," paint the most accurate picture of the situation which Scripture is describing.

That's quite a family setting! God is the King, in overall charge of the household. Pleasantness rules the home, and a song and a sense of completeness accompany daily life. What is more, they live in Bethlehem-Judah: "the House of Bread."

This idyllic scene was not to last however, as famine swept across Israel. Elimelech, saddened by his family's hunger, sought how to improve the situation and ensure that his family suffered no further.

Elimelech's first fatal error was in failing to realize that the difficulties they were facing were the consequences of spiritual, and not natural, problems. God had made clear His determination to lovingly provide for the children of Israel:

"...If thou shalt hearken diligently unto the voice of the Lord... and... do all His commandments... the Lord shall make thee plenteous in goods. But... if thou wilt not hearken unto the voice of the Lord... the fruit of thy land... shall a nation which thou knowest not eat up." (Deuteronomy 28:1, 11, 13 and 33)

There could only be one reason for famine in Israel: disobedience to God, and rebellion against His Word. That never seemed to strike Elimelech as he desperately considered his options. Finally, he decided on a plan. He would leave the House of Bread and journey, with his family, to a place called Moab. Possibly, in his time of deliberation, he had climbed into the high country around Bethlehem. From there he would have been able to see the plush, green pastures of Moab in the distance, and he decided that his best future lay there.

There was only one difficulty with Elimelech's plan. Moab means, "The land of no father." The Moabites were direct descendants of the children conceived by the incestuous relationship which the two daughters of Lot contrived to have with their father (Genesis 19:31-38). The very name "Moab" was anathema in Israel, and the law specifically forbade the entering of a Moabite into the congregation of the Lord (Deuteronomy 23:3). For Elimelech even to entertain the thought of going to Moab was a sign of unspeakable spiritual backsliding.

Fathers, you are the ones who, so often determine your family's future by the decisions you make. In God's name, don't ever decide based on income, without first considering the outcome.

Elimelech led his family on the journey away from the House of Bread, little knowing the tragedy that lay ahead. But then, tragedy goes hand-in-hand with decisions that we make apart from the will of God.

The route taken by the family very probably led them close to the still ruined walls of the city of Jericho.

"What happened here, father?" I can hear one of Elimelech's sons asking.

"Oh, this is where God did a mighty miracle when our forefathers first came to this land. God caused the walls to fall, and He delivered the city into the hands of the children of Israel."

"Why doesn't God do miracles now father? Why has He stopped doing mighty wonders for Israel?"

No answer.

A little later, they would find themselves passing the two piles of memorial stones, one at Gilgal, and the other close by at the River Jordan. "And this father, what are these for?" the other son might have asked.

"These were erected to commemorate the day that the Lord stopped the flow of the River Jordan when it was swollen with the spring floods. God allowed the children of Israel to pass across Jordan on dry land."

"God must have done many miracles, father. Why doesn't He do them now?

Again, no answer from Elimelech.

Eventually, the family reached Moab. They tried to settle down and just live like everyone else in Moab. The two sons even married Moabitish girls.

One day, Elimelech died. When you deliberately wander from God's will, you can be sure that it won't be long till the sense of God being King dies within your bosom. Soon to follow were the deaths of Mahlon and Chilion. The song had died and the sense of completeness was replaced by tragic emptiness.

The message could not be clearer. If, as fathers, you make decisions based only on materialistic ambitions or on an overriding concern for this world's treasures, you will be courting disaster. I cannot count the times I heard my father earnestly pray, "Lord, I don't care if I have to live in a tent, just make sure my family are all serving you." His one desire was for all his children to work full-time for God, and for no one with his blood to be left behind.

My father was anything but perfect, but I knew him better than anyone on Earth, and I knew that when he prayed like that, those weren't empty words.

If you want your family to walk on the streets of glory one day and call you blessed, don't get your priorities mixed up now. If a better job takes you away from the fellowship of the saints, let them keep it. If a certain deal will mean you having to compromise your Christian integrity, run from it. Little eyes are watching. They may not say a word, but you will never fool them.

"I'll Take What Daddy Takes"

I'm reminded of the story of a young boy whose mother had to be away one day, which meant that the little fellow had to spend the day at the office with Dad. The young boy occupied himself in a quiet corner while Dad took care of the day's business.

Lunchtime came, and Dad said, "Let's go for something to eat, son." Proudly, the young boy set off with his dad, so pleased to be sharing this special day.

Dad was his hero, and this was a day he would always remember.

At the restaurant, the waitress came to take their order. "What will you have to eat, sir?" she asked.

"Just the usual, thank you," replied the businessman.

"And for you?" she asked the boy.

"Oh, I'll take what Daddy takes," he beamed. "What will you have to drink, sir?" she queried, meaning an alcoholic beverage.

Uncomfortably, the man looked at his son for a moment, and then quickly answered: "Just the usual."

"What will you have, son?" the waitress asked.

The little boy smiled trustingly at his father, and again replied, "I'll take what Daddy takes."

The stark truth is that children all over the world have found themselves ending up in trouble, because all their lives they said, "I'll take what Daddy takes."

What are you taking, Daddy?

I know that this might be said of mothers too, but I am talking right now to the decision maker, the head of the home. If you don't decide for God, you may be condemning your children to a life of despair and an eternity in Hell. No double standards can be allowed. Many children end up hopelessly confused because what their parents say is often vastly different from what they do.

There is no getting away from it – the decisions that fathers make have eternal effects on their families. Whether those effects are bad or good depends on how the decisions were made. Ask yourself: "Will it glorify God? Would Jesus do it? Is it in line with what the Bible says? Does it hurt anyone? Will my family's spiritual life be impaired?"

Let those questions have precedence over, "How much will I make? Will I have a better house, a newer car, or a fancy office?"

Read Exodus 20:5 for a sobering thought: *"...I the Lord am a jealous God, visiting the iniquity of the fathers upon the children unto the third and fourth generation of them that hate me."*

I have not even addressed the many other horrendous possibilities of temptation to which fathers are uniquely vulnerable, but the stakes here are higher than every fortune on Earth put together. The souls of your children and loved ones are hanging in the balance! There's no choice. It must be God first.

Fathers, you must do everything possible to ensure that Christ is the reason for living in your home. It is your responsibility to ensure that everything you do as a family revolves around the person of Christ. When your kids see you unashamedly living for Christ and displaying a deep, intimate love relationship with Him, then they will be irrevocably influenced towards God.

Mothers and fathers sometimes fight with each other or let each other and their children down in various ways. No one can expect you to be perfect – but you can be real. My parents didn't always agree, but I've seen the laughter at the end of an argument, which made us children laugh as well.

Your children will not be attracted to a religion that makes you all smiles in church and a brute at home. Allow Christ to invade every part of your life? Give Him more of yourself each day, so that even when you make mistakes, your children will see your honest efforts to get things right. Let them witness that the value you place on walking with God is greater than any passing disagreement or mistake.

The promise of Household Salvation is yours, and no one can take it away. Even the devil cannot take it away. Receive it! Walk in it! Live it! IT'S TIME!

Chapter Eleven
God Is Never Late

—◈—

I have made much use in this book of the phrase, "IT'S TIME." I want now to show you from the Scriptures that God is always on time. He is never late, and no matter how bleak things may look now, help is already on the way.

You may be reading this book and not fully concentrating on it because worry consumes your mind over a loved one dear to you. Perhaps an unsaved husband is breaking your heart; or a teenage son or daughter is out on the town tonight, seeking pleasure, but risking disaster. Or it could be your wife who refuses to countenance the life you are leading, preferring to try to live a life without Christ.

Whatever your situation, I want you to take courage because IT'S TIME for God to move in your life.

My father lived an ungodly life, and for seven years put my mother through Hell while he was at it. It seemed that things were never going to get better. The more my mother prayed for him to get saved, the worse he got. Finally, when it seemed that she could not go any further when all hope was gone, God turned the situation around in one afternoon. Mum often says she discovered that God's permanent address is "Wits-End Corner." She was at the end of herself, but God was only just beginning to execute His purposes – in His precise and perfect timing. He is never late! He knows the beginning from the end, and He is the master-planner of the ages.

My mind turns to the story of Jonah, known by many as "the Reluctant Prophet." God had given him instructions to go to Nineveh and preach repentance to the city, but Jonah ran from the calling of God and booked himself passage on a ship. A great storm arose, and the ship's crew decided that Jonah was the cause of their troubles.

The Scripture says: *"So they took up Jonah, and cast him forth into the sea . . ."* (Jonah 1:15). Think of it for a moment. Poor old Jonah was out in the middle of the sea. There was a fearsome storm raging, and his shipmates had thrown him overboard. The ship, his only hope of ever seeing dry land again was sailing away.

The Bible says in Jeremiah: *"Behold, I am the Lord, the God of all flesh: is there anything too hard for me?"* (Jeremiah 32:27).

All flesh includes whale flesh, and I can hear the instructions going out to that whale as it swam the ocean depths. "Get yourself to these precise coordinates. Be near the surface and be there at the exact time I specify — don't be late! A man is going to drop into the sea, and I want you to swallow him, but *make sure you don't chew him*!"

Sounds crazy, doesn't it? But the story goes on: "Once you swallow him, swim the three-day journey to the beach at Nineveh. How does a whale know where Nineveh is? Swim up onto the dry land (not something you find whales doing very often), and spit the contents of your stomach on the beach."

I can't tell you how God did it. I only know that He did and that Jonah made it to Nineveh, even if he was slightly the worse for wear. The poor fellow would have been sucked pure white by the whale's gastric juices, and his hair would have been full of seaweed and fish bones. Little wonder that he had such a powerful impact on the awestruck Ninevites when he pushed his little white finger in front of their faces and gurgled, "Repent!"

God is never late! It was time for Jonah and it was time for Nineveh. When God wanted to accomplish His purposes, He let no obstacle, no whale, no storm and no reluctant prophet stand in His way.

Another incident involving a fish happened when the tax collectors came looking for the apostle Peter. (Matthew 17:24-27) The Lord told Peter to go down and cast in his hook and that the first fish to come up would have enough money in its mouth to pay their taxes. Impetuous Peter, must have felt a little strange carrying out that command. Can you see that little fish swimming to the seabed, picking up a coin of the exact value needed and then coming up toward the surface to look for Peter's hook? The fish had to be sure that it didn't get onto anyone else's hook. It had to be the right one. Beloved, God has always been on time, and in the matter of your family's salvation, He will be on time yet again.

What stirred in the hearts of the animals to cause them to make their way towards rescue in Noah's Ark? It is quite conceivable that the distances which some had to travel meant that they would have to reproduce, before dying on the way and let their young keep the appointment at the little wooden boat. If God can control the forces of nature in such a miraculous way, can we seriously doubt His ability to save our loved ones?

We find one of the most fascinating examples of God's perfect timing in the book of Esther. Two apparently unrelated events occur which later prove to be crucial in the unfolding plan of God. The first took place as the result of a drunken party in the palace of Ahasuerus, king of Persia. This king is identified in secular history as a despotic tyrant, who thought nothing of executing people for the slightest deviation from his wishes.

In his drunken state, the king ordered his beautiful queen, Vashti, to show herself before his guests. This was apparently intended to be a lewd and immodest display. The queen refused, and the king was left looking rather foolish before the assembled dignitaries. The king's counselors put pressure on him to make an example of the queen, and he weakly agreed and issued a decree removing her from her royal position. The vacancy created was filled by the lovely Esther, after an arranging of circumstances which only God could have performed. Esther was a Jewess, but that fact was hidden until much later.

Esther's guardian, Mordecai, then found himself involved in an incident which seemingly, was quite separate from the events which had taken place up until then. Mordecai overheard a plot to assassinate the king and duly reported it, allowing for the capture of the would-be assassins. We are told nothing more of the incident except that it was recorded in the national records.

Then, on the scene, appeared a man named Haman, a wicked, egotistical man, hungry for power. Haman was given a position of prime-ministerial importance, and the inhabitants of the land were commanded to bow in his presence. However, Mordecai the Jew refused to bow, indicating his determination to bow only to the God of Israel. The inflamed Haman then contrived a plan to convince the king that the Jews were his enemies and, once again, the king was swayed into issuing a decree. This time the order was for the total annihilation of the Jewish people. Decrees made by the Persian kings were irrevocable, so the situation for the Jews was critical and desperate.

In one of the most wonderful passages in all of Scripture, Mordecai sent for Queen Esther. As a Jewess, she would also suffer death if her origins were discovered. Esther was told that she must go before the king and plead for the lives of the Jewish people. That, however, was a dangerous task, since the penalty for going unbidden into the king's presence was death. Mordecai assured Esther of the necessity of taking the risk and spoke some strong words to her: *For if thou altogether holdest thy peace at this time, then shall their enlargement and deliverance arise to the Jews from another place: but thou and thy father's house shall be destroyed...* (Esther 4:14).

This verse continues with a question that you can ask yourself in your situation, as you believe God for your loved ones to be saved: *Who knoweth whether thou art come into the kingdom for such a time as this?*

The situation was desperate. The destruction of the Jewish nation was imminent unless something totally miraculous took place. That something was about to happen because of the boldness and faith of a little Jewish girl whom God had caused to become a queen.

After three days of fasting, Esther made her brave entrance into the presence of the unpredictable king. Mercifully, he stretched his scepter toward her, signifying that she would not be punished for this breach of court etiquette. It is a fact that serving God can often put us in some uncomfortable, unpredictable and even dangerous situations, but the spiritual destiny of so many souls may depend on our willingness to take the risk.

Esther's fortitude resulted in her being put into a position to incriminate the evil Haman. At the same time, Mordecai's previous service in saving the king's life was miraculously brought to the king's remembrance. Mordecai was honored, and Haman was hung on the very gallows which he had prepared for Mordecai. The Jews were given authority to defend themselves against anyone seeking to do them harm which, in effect, nullified the decree ordering their destruction.

The situation had been desperate. The danger was apparently irreversible ~ but God is never caught off guard. His preparation had been meticulous, His timing utterly impeccable. Read the whole book of Esther through for yourself if you want to be thrilled by the behind-the-scenes arranging of a God who never stops caring for His people.

Is your situation desperate? Does the problem seem irreversible to you? I want you to know, that though your loved ones may seem to be in the enemy's control,

God has every event monitored. He has every detail logged in His divine schedule for their lives.

Just as Esther was *"come into the kingdom for such a time as this,"* you too are caught up in the purposes of God. You are the secret weapon in your family that God will use to turn the impossible into a glorious living reality before your eyes.

God is not limited by the forces which limit us. Nature cannot limit Him. The decrees of a king cannot limit Him. He is the only one who really can make your dreams come true.

The stories we have discussed are all found in God's infallible Word, and the wonderful news is that He *"...is the same yesterday, today and forever"* (Hebrews 13:8). He never changes. He is always the same, and He wants your household to be saved.

IT'S TIME for your family. Your "anointed moment" is on the way. Watch for it, believe for it ~ IT'S TIME.

Chapter Twelve

It's Time

—m—

In Psalm 78, the writer recounts some events from the journey of the children of Israel through the wilderness. We learn that despite the many blessings and the miraculous provision which the children of Israel experienced, they were still riddled with unbelief – so much so that they asked the question: *"Can God furnish a table in the wilderness?"* (Psalm 78:19).

I want you to know, that even though it may seem to you, in your situation that you are going through a wilderness experience, God *can* spread His table of provision for you!

Unbelief blinded the children of Israel. They had seen miracle after miracle, still, they persisted to doubt God. They had seen fresh manna fall every day, to feed them. God sent them quail because they complained that they had no meat. They drank every day – in the desert – from the rock that followed them. Like the children of Israel, we today have been mightily blessed of God. What we cannot afford to do is to doubt that our God will come through for us in our wilderness.

Your family circumstances may seem like a wilderness situation now, but God will always spread a table for those who trust in Him!

There is a wonderful story in Genesis Chapter 21 which I need to share with you:

Abraham had been blessed by the birth of Isaac, finally receiving the son God had promised him. Due to his previous impatience, he had already become father to another son, Ishmael, by his wife's maid, Hagar.

After a time, Abraham's wife, Sarah, saw Ishmael mocking the young Isaac. That was all the protective mother needed to insist that Ishmael and his mother Hagar be thrust out – *into the wilderness.* The only provisions given to them were some bread and a bottle of water. Soon these were used up, and their hopelessness was expressed in the phrase: *"And the water was spent in the bottle"* (Genesis 21:15).

They were in the wilderness, and out of water. I think it would be hard to imagine a more dangerous situation than they faced. Whatever difficulty you may be in, whatever the problem you may be facing in trying to win your loved ones to Christ, your situation can be no more impossible than that of Hagar and Ishmael.

Though their circumstances were dire, God made a promise to the young Ishmael, that he too would be the father of a mighty nation. As Hagar lifted her voice, wept, and prepared to die, God intervened and began to spread a table in the wilderness for them. The Bible says: *"And God opened her eyes, and she saw a well of water"* (Genesis 21:19). God didn't just give them another *bottle of water,* God gave them *a whole well of water!* It was a practically limitless supply, to meet all their future needs.

Do you feel you are in the wilderness? Does it seem that your resources are dried up, and you've spent all the water in your bottle? If so, then you are in a perfect position for God to spread a table for you, and show you the well of water flowing to meet your need!

Throughout history, there have been many times when it seemed that mankind was in a spiritual wilderness; when it appeared that the water in the bottle was spent. There are so many instances in the Old Testament alone that we could not possibly go into them all in detail, but the stories of God intervening amid a spiritual wilderness have thrilled Christians for centuries.

Time after time, in the book of Judges, for instance, God answered the cries of His people with help and deliverance. Where there had been idolatry and sin, God spread a table in the wilderness and sent rescuers—men and women anointed by the Holy Spirit.

Of all the times when there has been mass spiritual blindness and barrenness in this world, none could have been more desperate than a period around two thousand years ago. The prophets had been silent for four hundred years. No one, it seemed, had a word from the Lord, but God always knows when IT'S TIME.

The people began to speak about a strange man dressed in camel's hair, who lived on a diet of locusts and wild honey. There was something about his voice too: it was as the voice of one crying *in the wilderness, "Prepare ye the way of the Lord, make His paths straight"* (Mark 1:3).

When there was no voice, God raised up a voice in the wilderness, to let mankind know that the Savior of the world would soon appear. It was time to spread a table. It was time to open a well of water from which men could drink, and never thirst again. *But whosoever drinketh of the water that I shall give him shall never thirst; but the water that I shall give him shall be in him a well of water, springing up into everlasting life* (John 4:14).

It was time to redeem mankind. Scripture says: *But when the fullness of time was come, God sent forth His Son...* (Galatians 4:4). The only begotten Son of God took on human form and lived among the sons of men. Then, after thirty-three short years, three of which He spent healing, blessing and changing all who would receive from Him, the most awesome moment in history arrived. *My time is at hand,* He said (Matthew 26:8).

They took the spotless Lamb of God, God's Son, and with cruel, filthy hands, they nailed Him naked to a tree. They made Him a barbed crown of lance-like thorns and pressed it mercilessly into the flesh of His head. They tore the beard from His face and spat on Him. Their hatred was so great, so awful was the wilderness of sin in which they had become entangled. His back was like a plowed field from the malicious whipping that they had subjected Him to.

Speaking prophetically of Christ, God said in Isaiah 52:14, *His visage was so marred more than any man and His form more than the sons of men."* In other words, He was barely recognizable as a human being by the time they finished savaging Him. Little wonder that the sun would not shine, but rather refused to have any part in such a display of unspeakable horror.

He hung there without complaint. The hymn tells us that *"He could have called ten thousand angels to destroy this world, and to set Him free."* In His final throes of agony, He declared, *"It is finished,"* and He gave up the ghost (John 19:30). He died.

They took Him down and laid Him in a borrowed tomb. Think of it! They placed God's Son in a grave that belonged to someone else. His disciples mourned for three days as they tried to reconcile themselves to the realization that all their dreams lay buried in the tomb with Him. But they were unaware of what was happening. The hour had finally arrived on the divine timepiece of the ages. I can imagine the call God reverberating through the corridors of Heaven, 'That's enough! The price for sin has been paid! ~ IT'S TIME!"

All the demons of Hell must have gathered in that tomb to mock gleefully at their victory over the second Adam. But their glee must have turned to despair. For Jesus descended into Hell and took the keys of death,

Hell, and the grave. God said, "IT'S TIME," and Jesus arose from the dead, having conquered the power of sin forever.

There has been no greater wilderness than when all of mankind was condemned under the power of sin. When it was time, God provided the ultimate answer. The shed blood of Christ nullified the effects of sin's wilderness forever. The water in the bottle was spent, but the well of salvation sprung open, and we still drink from its endless supply today! Salvation still flows like a river. Allow it flow into your heart, the barriers will break, and your loved ones will find themselves swept along by the force of the tide. IT'S TIME.

History, since that momentous occasion, has continuously shown that whenever one found himself faced with a spiritual wilderness, God spreads a table.

It was during the great Reformation, under Martin Luther, when centuries of darkness were swept away. The Church again began to realize that *the just shall live by faith.*

That Reformation spread to my homeland of Scotland through a man named John Knox, who prayed, "Give me Scotland or I die." God answered his prayer and most of the population of Scotland, at that time, came to a saving knowledge of Jesus Christ. I pray with all my heart for such a revival to sweep through Scotland again, for right now it is in a deep spiritual wilderness. Today it's time for your loved ones. It's also time for a mighty outpouring in Scotland. One day you'll hear, on your daily news broadcast: "We don't know what's happening in Scotland, except that there has been an amazing spiritual awakening, and the nation is turning to God once again." Pray with me about that—IT'S TIME for Scotland.

In England, God used two brothers named John and Charles Wesley to spread a table in the wilderness. The spiritual revival they helped launch averted the bloody slaughter of the French revolution from spreading across the channel to England.

The truth of water baptism by immersion was another table in the wilderness. In the United States, the Pentecostal outpouring at Azusa Street was another. God has always been on time. He is never late. Whenever the wilderness threatened to choke the spiritual life in mankind, God always spread a table.

You may feel you are in a wilderness. Perhaps you feel that sin is prevailing on every corner, be it alcoholism, drugs, prostitution, or whatever. You may feel like a tiny voice crying in such a vast wilderness. Whether you live in North America, Great Britain, or elsewhere, you know the extent of the spiritual wilderness around you.

The Word of God has something to say about these times: *"In the last days, saith God, I will pour out my Spirit upon all flesh "*(Acts 2:17). We are about to see the climax of the ages, as this dispensation of time ends. But before that happens, all Heaven is going to be let loose. *"The time is at hand,"* the Bible says (Revelation 22:10).

If you have unsaved loved ones, they are flesh too and therefore subject to this last day outpouring of God's precious Holy Spirit. IT'S TIME for North America. IT'S TIME for Scotland. IT'S TIME for the United Kingdom. IT'S TIME for *the world!* IT'S TIME for God to roll back the wilderness in your family, and spread the table of full Household Salvation. That wayward son or daughter is in your field. God won't let you lose him or her to the devil. That wife, that husband, those loved ones you have prayed for so long are about to discover that IT'S TIME for them too. IT'S TIME for Household Salvation. No matter how entangled your loved ones may be in sin's wilderness, God has said that *"thou shalt be saved and thy house. "*God will bring them in. He is about to astound you by the marvelous, mighty way in which He will cause salvation to come to your household.

If your family's salvation has never concerned you, it is now time to be concerned. If you have been concerned, but have been getting discouraged, now is the time to take heart, for there is a well of water about to spring up in the wilderness for you. Believe His Word ~ claim the unclaimed promise. IT'S TIME for Household Salvation.

Conclusion

The truth of Household Salvation has, as I have shared with you, changed my life and ministry. I have a burning desire to challenge as many as possible to begin to trust God for their families.

It has been three decades or more since I sat in my office and witnessed the horrors of Hell in the vision that so changed my life. Twenty-five years ago, something else happened that brought even more drastic change to my life and ministry. No longer was God asking me to believe for the children that were mine alone, but He challenged me to believe for children who had no one to stand for them. The orphan, those souls created by death or abandonment wasting in institutions. The message of Household Salvation can have a greater impact in your life than you can ever imagine. Today these abandoned orphans have been transformed into sons and daughters who are now partners with me in a ministry that is transforming other orphans. Along with my own family, these amazing kids have become an extension of the passion I held in my heart so many years ago. The promise from God that He would save my whole family has been extended into the orphanage and multiple families of orphaned children, brothers, sisters, and cousins have come to find reality of Jesus, peace and grace to return to the very people who abandoned them in the orphanage. To watch this truth be manifest in my own family is an amazing thing. To see it manifest in the life of an orphan is truly the greatest act of grace I have ever witnessed. Your family is not beyond the grip of grace. There is not a pigpen built that can hold your son or daughter. There is nothing, NOTHING that can separate you from His love or His promise. Speaketh with me now "As for me and my house, we will SERVE the Lord."

I know the difference it makes to be part of an entire family who love Jesus and who want their lives to be used to glorify Him. I hope that as I have shared with you how God moved amongst the Camerons, you have seen the wonderful possibilities in your life.

Nothing will influence your family more than if the Christianity you preach is the Christianity you live. If Christ is all-important to you, then the enthusiasm of your unreserved love for Him will captivate your loved ones as it has captivated you. I'm believing with you for your family's salvation, but I cannot overstate how important it is that you are real with God and real with your family. Be "naturally spiritual" and "spiritually natural." Don't put on a front. Don't put on your "religious voice" every time your family comes into the room. Be yourself, in love with Jesus, and you'll do more than you could ever do by constantly "preaching" at your family.

God is about to sweep through the Church with a tremendous outpouring of Household Salvation. It won't be just individuals coming to Christ, but whole families will be ushered into the Kingdom.

IT'S TIME for this outpouring to begin, and you need to be a part of it. Be instant in prayer; read and re-read the God's wonderful promises to you. Don't ever give up expecting God to move in your family!

IT'S TIME for your house to come to Christ. IT'S TIME FOR HOUSEHOLD SALVATION! IT'S TIME. IT'S TIME. IT'S TIME!

 If you have unsaved loved ones for whom you'd like Philip & Chrissie to join with you in prayer, please write their names here (you only need their first name) and their relationship to you.

The Orphan's Hands, P.O. Box 242248, Montgomery, AL 36124.

For prayer call: 1-334-866-0069

Philip & Chrissie, please pray for my loved ones:

_____ _____

_____ _____

_____ _____

_____ _____

_____ _____

_____ _____

_____ _____

_____ _____

Full House